SPECIAL PAPERS IN INTERNATIONAL ECONOMICS

No. 5, SEPTEMBER 1963

THE BALANCE ON FOREIGN TRANSACTIONS: PROBLEMS OF DEFINITION AND MEASUREMENT

WALTHER LEDERER

INTERNATIONAL FINANCE SECTION

DEPARTMENT OF ECONOMICS

PRINCETON UNIVERSITY · 1963

Printed in the United States of America by Princeton University Press
at Princeton, New Jersey

TABLE OF CONTENTS

The Balance on Foreign Transactions: Problems of Definition and Measurement

I. Introduction

Compilations of the balance of international transactions include data on all transfers of real resources and financial assets between residents of one country and those of others. They are historic records, based on a double-entry-bookkeeping principle. Each transaction appears twice in the accounts, with a credit entry and a debit entry, both in exactly the same magnitude. Thus, if goods are exported and payment is received in the form of a check drawn against an account of a foreign resident in a U.S. bank, the credit entry would be merchandise exports, the debit entry the corresponding decline in U.S. liabilities to foreigners, since checking accounts held by foreign residents in U.S. banks constitute a liability of that bank.

If the exports are not paid for in the same accounting period, because the payment has been deferred by a loan, the debit entry would be an "outflow" of U.S. capital; if the exports are provided as a gift, the debit entry would be called a gift or "unilateral transfer." No matter what form the financial arrangement may take, there always has to be a debit entry equal to the value of the exports.

If each transaction is represented by equal credit and debit entries, the total of all transactions must be represented by equal totals for all credits and all debits. Except for the fact that statistical data for international transactions are not complete and estimates may be off the mark, the two sides of the balance sheet always have to be equal.

By dividing all of the balance-of-payments items into two groups, each of the two will balance to the same figure with opposite signs. The figures themselves never indicate that one of these two groups is the cause, the other the effect. In fact, the number of potential groupings is quite large. If one attempts to read cause-effect relationships into such groupings, they represent hypotheses which are not based on the balance-of-payments data themselves, but on other assumptions. These assumptions, however, are not subject to proof or disproof on the basis of balance-of-payments statistics, and the number of such

5

hypotheses is potentially as large as the number of groupings into which the entire compilation can be divided.

The setting-up of categories, distinguishing between them with respect to their significance, calling attention to certain balances rather than to others, is thus a matter of interpretation of the data, analysis of the relationships between the various transactions, and the relationships of these transactions to other economic and sometimes non-economic developments, conditions, and policy goals. The analysis will necessarily vary with the purpose for which it is made.

It should be expected, therefore, that differences arise among analysts with respect to the interpretations of the data and the conclusions drawn from them. Some of these differences, however, indicate not really contradictory positions; instead, they are due to differences in the problems for which answers are sought, not to differences in answers to the same problem.

Neither the apparent nor the real conflicts in the interpretations of compilations of international transactions would be particularly disturbing if the discussion of balance-of-payments problems were only among the relatively few specialists in that field and had only theoretical interest. In most other countries in the free world, and for some years now also in the United States, the balance-of-payments problem has arisen as a subject of national concern, a major issue requiring public-policy formulation, and consequently has attracted growing interest among large sections of the population.

It is important, therefore, that the problems of analyzing the data be better understood. This requires not only the clarification of the purpose for which the analysis is intended, but also some knowledge of what the figures represent. In this paper it is attempted to set out some of the considerations in finding a focus for the analysis, to define that focus in terms of specific types of transactions, and to examine the statistical data and institutional conditions of the United States in order to determine which of the data best meet this purpose. The paper discusses also alternative concepts used by other analysts, and attempts to explain the reasons for the differences.

II. The Need for Balance-of-Payments Statistics: A Recent Development

1. *Early Interest Mainly Academic*

Perhaps the first approach to balance-of-payments statistics could be made by asking what is the purpose of such statistics, and when and why a need for them has arisen. An answer to these questions may, perhaps, help in singling out one or more types of analytical approaches which may make these statistics useful in the evaluation of past economic developments and as a tool in economic-policy formulation.

In the United States the interest in balance-of-payments statistics has only recently developed. In most other countries such interest arose much earlier. Even there, however, the use of such statistics in policy formulations by government or central-bank authorities hardly goes back before the 1930's, and in most countries it only started during or after World War II. Before that time, apparently, balance-of-payments statistics were not considered essential, although many countries had progressed to their present state of economic and financial development and although their international transactions were about as varied and intensive, relative to the size of their economies, as they are now.

This does not mean, however, that no balance-of-payments statistics were compiled. The interest in such statistics, however, was mainly theoretical and illustrative to provide examples of the different types of international transactions and their magnitude during a selected time period, and to show the movements in those particular items that were considered international reserves and means for international settlements.

Balance-of-payments data over longer periods of time were also used to show the longer-run changes in certain items and their interrelationships, as for instance in connection with the problem of economic development of a country and of a change in its position from international debtor to international creditor.

The compilations of balance-of-payments statistics in the United States date back to the years immediately following World War I. They were started as a result of the problems created by the large

7

loans which the United States gave its allies to finance their expenditures abroad (mostly in the United States), and of the problems of financing their postwar reconstruction. In Germany, interest in the balance of payments was greatly stimulated by the problems created by the transfer of reparations. Balance-of-payments data were used to expose the requisites for such transfers and the difficulties involved, but not necessarily to guide policy with respect to international reserves.

If countries once were able to get along without specific use of balance-of-payments statistics and to progress to a state of economic development not much different from that of the western world today—including highly diversified industrial economies operating with modern financial methods and linked with other countries through widespread real and financial exchanges—what has changed to make the use of balance-of-payments statistics indispensable as a guide for policy formulation?

2. The Influence of Changing Institutions

The principal changes are probably the separation of domestic and international liquidity considerations; the transfer of responsibility for the latter from the banking systems to the governments; and the attempts by the governments to pursue economic policies within each of the several countries independent of economic relationships to the rest of the world, and yet to maintain more or less fixed exchange relationships of their own currencies with those of other countries or with a recognized international medium of exchange, such as the U.S. dollar or gold. What matters here is the combination of these policies. Pursuing domestic economic policies independently of international economic relationships by isolating the domestic monetary system from the effects of reserve accumulations or reductions, or if necessary by changing exchange rates—a widespread practice during the interwar period, particularly the latter half—does not require balance-of-payments data as policy guides.[1] Only if the policy also includes the maintenance of stable foreign-exchange rates, do the transactions associated with changes in international liquidity become subject to direct or indirect policy actions, and data on the size of these transactions and understanding of the forces affecting them become essential.

[1] The operations of Exchange Stabilization Funds were analyzed by Ragnar Nurkse in *International Currency Experience* (League of Nations, 1944), chapter VI.

As long as private commercial banks, or even the central banks (which in some instances were in fact private banks themselves or central institutions organized by and for the commercial banks), did not distinguish between their domestic and foreign business, they did not have to distinguish between domestic and foreign assets and liabilities.

They generally followed the policy of keeping their less liquid higher-yield assets as large as possible without endangering their financial solvency.[2] To ensure this solvency they would keep their more liquid lower-yield assets in such ratios to their demand liabilities as they considered necessary to provide a safe margin.

What constituted a liquid asset depended upon its acceptance as a means of settling debts between banks and their creditors, including other banks, or such assets as could quickly be converted into acceptable means of settlement with a minimum loss of value.

In the absence of a central bank (whether established by the government or by usage), liquid assets of banks would have been gold. As central banks were established, or certain metropolitan banks developed into the position of bankers' banks, deposits in these banks or their notes served as liquid or reserve assets for other banks, provided the former assumed the obligation—and could clearly meet it—to convert their notes into gold. This, in fact, ensured the complete convertibility of national into international media of exchange, as was pointed out by Robert Triffin.[3]

Deposits in such banks, or their notes, served then as substitute for, or supplement to, gold as a medium for settling obligations and as a form of liquid asset which could be used as reserve assets against demand obligations by other banks, enterprises, or persons.

Since the notes and deposits created by these reserve banks were generally considered to be essentially a stand-in for gold—with gold remaining the ultimate means of settlement and ultimate reserve asset—the liabilities of the reserve banks were limited by their desire to pre-

[2] The term "financial solvency," as used here, refers to the ability of a debtor to pay claims against him when they are due. This implies that the debtor has sufficient amounts of "cash" (i.e. assets acceptable to others as a medium of exchange) on hand, or that he has liquid assets which can be converted into cash with a minimum of delay and loss in value. Financial solvency may be distinguished from total solvency, which means that the fair value of the total assets of the debtor (given a reasonable time for liquidation or assuming a reasonable capitalization of his earning assets) equal or exceed his debts.

[3] "The Return to Convertibility: 1926-1931 and 1958- ? or Convertibility and the Morning After," Banca Nazionale del Lavoro, *Quarterly Review* (Rome, March 1959), pp. 6ff.

serve their financial solvency, that is, their ability to convert notes and deposits into gold whenever required.

The establishment in each of the various countries of central-reserve banks in which the other banks kept their reserves reduced the need for internationally acceptable assets, such as gold, for purposes of settlement of claims within each of these countries. The money supplies used in domestic circulation could be raised relative to the available reserves in international assets as long as the central-reserve banks stood ready—and were trusted—to convert upon demand their own liabilities (that is, their notes and deposits held there by the commercial banks) into international cash assets. As long as the central-reserve bank in each country followed the policy of safeguarding its own solvency, the international solvency of the country, in the sense of its ability to preserve the exchange value of its currency, was ensured.

Metropolitan banks, which were located in countries carrying on a large amount of foreign trade or able to provide financial resources to others, and which at the same time were considered to be sheltered from outside interference with their business operations, particularly with respect to their own financial solvency, developed into bankers' banks not only within their own country but for other countries as well.

The world-wide monetary system has thus been further enlarged, to the extent that private as well as central-reserve banks in each of the various countries keep as part of their own reserves such claims as deposits in the banks of a reserve-currency country. This gold-exchange standard depends upon the confidence that these claims are convertible into gold as long as gold is considered the ultimate medium of international payments.[4]

The higher up on the reserve pyramid a bank happens to be, the greater is its responsibility in this type of monetary system, and the more careful it has to be in safeguarding its own currency. This is sometimes accomplished by keeping higher reserve ratios, by reacting faster to changes in its reserve position, or by pursuing a more active policy to prevent such changes than would be required by banks on a lower level of the monetary pyramid.

Provided, then, each layer of bank—from the local level through the

[4] The use of foreign exchange for monetary reserves of central banks before World War I was quite small. In 1913, foreign exchange accounted for less than 10 percent of central-bank reserve assets. The gold-exchange standard became more prevalent in the 1920's. In 1928 foreign exchange comprised about one-fourth of central-bank reserves, and outside the United States and the United Kingdom about 38 percent. (See Triffin, *op.cit.*, p. 24.)

various reserve levels—makes sure to preserve its financial solvency, there is no difference between domestic and international solvency of the banking and currency systems. An inflow of internationally acceptable cash (gold or deposits in a recognized large bank in a country whose currency is accepted for international transactions) provides the base for the recipient bank to issue its own notes or deposits and thus to increase the money supply in its own country. An outflow of international cash forces the bank to reduce its own liabilities, and thus the money supply in its country shrinks.

The ratio between cash reserves and demand obligations of a bank depends upon the judgment of the amount and speed of withdrawals of cash relative to receipts of new deposits, the ability to reduce withdrawals of funds or to attract new funds, and to liquidate loans and investments or obtain credit to meet an unforeseen excess of cash withdrawals. The higher the customary ratio between deposit and similar obligations to reserves, the more an inflow or outflow of internationally acceptable cash will affect the size of a country's banking deposits and notes, and thus its money supply.[5] This will affect its economy, stimulating it, if the money supply increases, or constricting it if it declines.

Provided a country's standing in international trade and its attractiveness for capital investments is roughly equal to that of competing countries, the changes in money supply, and correspondingly in incomes and demands, will tend to counteract the forces which caused the changes in the country's assets in international reserves. This will be greatly facilitated if the banking system reacts quickly to changes in its liquidity position, and the forces which are responsible for these changes are counteracted before they can ramify and become strongly entrenched in the economy. Quick reactions will tend to maintain the country's competitive position and, therefore, minimize the drain on its reserves. A policy of maintaining reserves close to the required amount is often more effective in that respect than one which permits accumulations and reductions of excess reserves, because the latter policy will facilitate postponement of needed actions.

Except in those cases where a country's competitive position is seriously impaired by developments beyond its control, a decline in its reserves of international cash assets may affect the solvency of indi-

[5] To keep the reserve ratio constant, the absolute change in the domestic money supply has to be a multiple of the change in reserves by the inverse of that ratio, but, relatively, the change in the money supply will be the same as in reserves.

vidual enterprises, but it will not affect the exchange value of its currency, as long as the banks themselves—at least those whose obligations are used in international transactions—preserve their own financial solvency, or the necessary ratio of liquid assets to demand liabilities. Thus the normal desire of the private banks and enterprises to maintain their solvency—which is just as important to preserve their ability to continue in operation as earning a return on their investment (and in the short run even more important)—will ensure the exchange value of a country's currency, and thus make it unnecessary for the government to take special actions to accomplish that.

International liquidity becomes a problem to the government when the government itself takes actions to relieve banks and the monetary authority of their country from the requirement of keeping their reserves in internationally acceptable assets and permits (or forces) them to substitute as reserve assets obligations of the government itself. In many countries, including the United States and the United Kingdom, the governments have taken over the international assets. Even where that has not been done, the independence of the central banks to follow their own policy of maintaining international liquidity and their ability to counteract or resist policies by their government is subject to doubt. In countries where the effective authority of the governments over the central banks and the rest of the banking system has been established—and most countries in the western world have accepted that political relationship—the task of maintaining international liquidity and the exchange value of their currencies has become the final responsibility of the governments. The more or less simple guidelines which banks and central banks have used for maintaining their international solvency—and thereby for safeguarding the exchange rate of the currency—have not been accepted by the governments in order to reduce the restraints imposed on domestic economic activity by the banking policy of maintaining fixed ratios between external reserves and the domestic money supply.

This development is stated here as a historic fact. It is neither deplored nor considered desirable. It has historic reasons and it is outside of the scope of this paper to judge whether the historic events with which this expansion in governmental authority and responsibility was associated left no other alternative to meet the problems created by them, and whether the same or other reasons force governments to continue this function.

12

III. Changes in International Liquidity as a Focus of Balance-of-Payments Analysis

1. *Interpreting Balance-of-Payments Statistics*

If governments want to meet the responsibility of maintaining the exchange value of their currencies, they require certain guidelines to substitute for those used by the banks in their effort to conduct their business within the limits imposed by considerations of financial solvency.

Balance-of-payments compilations and their analysis are supposed to be among such guidelines. The question is how the data should be interpreted to meet this purpose. This does not imply that balance-of-payments data could not also be used for other purposes, but such other uses are not being considered here. Neither does it mean that the balance of payments should be the only guideline to economic policy.

(a) General equilibrium versus exchange equilibrium

Several conditions which are implicit in the use of balance-of-payments compilations as a policy guide to public officials in their task of maintaining the exchange value of their currency may be reemphasized.

Changes in international liquidity could not serve as a focus of balance-of-payments analysis if it were the policy to let the exchange value fluctuate freely and to permit the demand and supply of the currency in the international exchange market to be equated through exchange-rate adjustments. In this case, reserves of internationally acceptable media of payment (except perhaps for major national emergencies) would not be needed, and the size of domestic liabilities of the banking system, and the domestic money supply, could be completely independent of the availability of external cash assets.

Under such conditions, international transactions would be in balance without net transfers of international cash assets. Differences in the movements of supply and demand would appear in changes of exchange rates, which are not shown in balance-of-payments statements. Changes in exchange rates, however, would have repercussions on the international transactions themselves and affect their magnitude. The latter would appear in balance-of-payments compilations, and

13

judgments concerning the desirability of these changes might provide the basis for policy decisions.

Focusing the analysis of the balance of payments of a country on changes in its international liquidity implies that economic conditions within that country as they are affected by its economic relations with the rest of the world are moved into the center of the examination. This is different from focusing on equilibrium in the exchange market. Equilibrium in the exchange market does not necessarily imply equilibrium in the economic conditions of the countries whose currencies (which are its monetary liabilities) are traded in the market. This distinction applies to the foreign-exchange market as much as to any other market. The mere fact that supply and demand are equated, does not mean that at the established market price each individual seller or buyer has to be in equilibrium. If any of them are not, they will have to change their production and marketing policies. Likewise, equilibrium in the exchange market may have been obtained through the establishment of conditions which in the long run cannot be continued. The equilibrium in the exchange market under such conditions will not coincide with an equilibrium in the country's own economy and in its international economic relationships. An analysis focusing on equilibrium in the exchange market, therefore, would be deficient as a policy guide to monetary authorities.

On the other hand, changes in international liquidity are not a sufficient measure of equilibrium in a country's international economic relationship, any more than changes in its liquidity provide a complete guide to the equilibrium of a single enterprise.

(b) International versus domestic equilibrium

In the case of an enterprise, equilibrium in its operations can be assumed to exist if it has maximized its profits and established and maintained an optimum amount of liquidity, so that, as long as conditions over which it has no control continue, no changes in its operations are required. The combination of these criteria is also applicable to the operations of central banks, or banking systems as a whole, provided they operate on the basis of private enterprises. They will keep their lending at the highest point consistent with a safe international liquidity. When international liquidity increases, lending can be expanded; if it declines, loans outstanding have to be curtailed. Expansion and curtailment of loans have some effect on the money supply and the general level of business activity in the country, and set in motion developments which counteract and ultimately correct

14

the original change in international liquidity. This at least is the simplified pattern underlying private-banking responsibility for international liquidity, although the ideal conditions required for a successful functioning of this adjustment mechanism may never have existed. While this system does tend to provide the mechanism to ensure the continued operation of the banking system, including the central bank, it does not necessarily ensure the optimum rate of operation of the economy as a whole.

Relieving the banks of responsibility for the maintenance of international liquidity and transferring it to the government makes it necessary to develop another yardstick for equilibrium. The principle of maximizing profits cannot be applied to the nation. A reasonable substitute, however, might be the principle of maximizing the real income of the nation. This principle would have to be combined with the principle of maintaining international liquidity at the optimum level.

From this it follows that maintaining international liquidity, at whatever level it happens to be, does not necessarily indicate that a country's position relative to the rest of the world is in equilibrium. Its economy may be operating at a rate which is less than that which would maximize the real incomes of its residents. If the rise in output and income is avoided because it is feared that it may impinge on the country's international liquidity, then the measure of international disequilibrium will really be the estimated amount of loss in liquidity that would occur if the operations of the economy were expanded to the maximum. Policies to restore the level of output to the maximum permitted with the available resources would have to concentrate on measures strengthening the country's competitive position in the international markets for goods and services, and its attractiveness for capital investments—essentially the same measures which would have to be taken if the country actually had suffered a decline in liquidity.[1]

[1] Essentially the same view was expressed by Ragnar Nurkse in "Conditions of International Monetary Equilibrium" Essays of International Finance, No. 4 (International Finance Section, Princeton University, Spring 1945), quoted from reprint in American Economic Association, Readings in the Theory of International Trade (The Blakiston Company: Philadelphia-Toronto, 1949), pp. 11 and 12. "At different levels of national income and employment in a given country, equilibrium in the balance of payments can be secured at different rates of exchange. It would seem better therefore to define the true equilibrium rate of exchange as one that maintains a country's external accounts in equilibrium without the need for wholesale unemployment at home. And if we extend our view from the position of a single country to the whole network of international exchange rates this would lead us to define an ideal system of equilibrium rates as one that main-

This definition of equilibrium makes it theoretically possible that all economies are out of equilibrium in the same direction; for instance, if they are operating in varying degrees at less than capacity but without changes in their international liquidity position. Each of the countries may hesitate to expand production because of a potentially adverse effect on its reserves.

This example does not show that the requirements for international equilibrium in a country, as stated above, are potentially absurd, but that internationally as well as within a country (particularly if one assumes a closed economy, which the world economy indeed is) productive resources are not necessarily always utilized to the optimum extent. Under conditions of general underutilization of productive capacities, individual enterprises—and countries—frequently tend to enlarge their liquidity by restricting their operations rather than to expand their activity by putting more of their liquid funds into productive investments.

In this case the disequilibrium may not only be partial but also universal. This means, in effect, that even if the international exchange markets are in balance, and changes in international liquidity are minimized, the world economy can be out of equilibrium. Policy changes are then required, but to be effective those attempted within each of the separate countries may have to be supplemented by measures taken cooperatively by all, or at least the major, countries. This cooperation can, of course, be facilitated through international organizations, such as the International Monetary Fund.

In the course of a general expansion in the world economy it would become apparent whether international liquidities can be maintained by all countries or whether some may have to take further measures to achieve both an optimum level of output and optimum international liquidity.

(c) Changes in international liquidity

Another reason why stability in a country's international liquidity may not reflect international equilibrium for a country's economy can be the lack of reserves (or borrowing facilities) with which to

---

tains the accounts of all countries simultaneously in equilibrium when all countries simultaneously are free from mass unemployment on the one hand and inflation on the other." A similar point was made by E. M. Bernstein in "Strategic Factors in Balance of Payments Adjustment," *The Review of Economics and Statistics*, Vol. XL, Supplement (February 1958), pp. 133ff. See also the following discussion of Bernstein's paper by Fritz Machlup, *ibid*, pp. 137ff.

finance all, or part, of an excess of its demand for foreign exchange over receipts from regular transactions. The country may be operating at, or close to, the maximum rate, but with the supply of foreign exchange not meeting the demand, the free market for foreign exchange is replaced by governmental rationing of the available supply, or by exchange controls. Neither the foreign-exchange market nor the balance of payments affords a measurement of the disequilibrium under such conditions. The only indication of disequilibrium at unchanged exchange rates may be found in the rise in the backlog of unsatisfied demand for foreign exchange and of overdue obligations to foreigners. Under different exchange rates, of course, these magnitudes would be different.[2]

If any part of the unsatisfied demand for foreign exchange is met from extraordinary sources, such as grants or loans by foreign governments, the amount of such funds utilized does not measure the *ex ante* disequilibrium either, but merely that portion which the country *ex post* has been able to meet in such manner.[3]

The conditions under which changes in international liquidity alone can be used as a measure of international equilibrium include, therefore, operation of the economy at the maximum level compatible with the resources at its disposal and reserves or credit facilities ample enough to permit the prevailing demand for foreign exchange to be met without restrictions.

One of the conditions of equilibrium of the country—as has been stated above—is that international liquidity is kept at an optimum level. What should be considered as optimum—the most desirable point—depends upon the prospective need for reserves which, in turn, depends upon an estimate of the potential gap between payments and receipts from its initial appearance until it is likely to be closed again.

The gap may be due to political, natural, and economic develop-

[2] See Nurkse, *op.cit.*, p. 9.

[3] Foreign aid as a measure of the balance in international transactions has been used by the International Monetary Fund as part of the concept of compensatory financing. (*Balance of Payments Yearbook 1938, 1946, 1947.*) It was also used in an article by Paul Host-Madsen, Chief of the Balance of Payments Division of the IMF, to measure changes in world payments imbalances in the postwar period. "Measurements of Imbalances in World Payments 1947-58," *Staff Papers*, Vol. IX, No. 3 (November 1962). The distinction between *ex ante* market or program balance, and the *ex post* accounting balance, as well as the inconsistencies involved in the concepts used by the IMF at that time, are stressed by Fritz Machlup in "Three Concepts of the Balance of Payments," *Economic Journal*, Vol. LX (March 1950).

ments. It also depends, however, upon whether the country decides to keep its own economy operating in the same manner as before the developments which opened the gap (for example, to maintain a free market economy at or near the capacity level of operation), or to make adjustments to reduce foreign expenditures toward the point where they match current receipts. The need for reserves is reduced, however, by the availability of special credits from other countries, or from international organizations.

Evaluations of the prospects of these conditions and their impact do not remain static, of course, and the requirements for reserves are likely to change. A country may find itself short of reserves, and may attempt to set up policies through its monetary authorities to increase its international liquidity. The opposite development may persuade monetary authorities that the country's international liquidity is higher than required, and that foreign expenditures of the country can be permitted to expand to absorb the excess reserves. In other words, changes in international reserves—or liquidity—should not be considered a passive result of other—"autonomous"—transactions, but can be the object of conscious and purposeful policy of the monetary authorities; the acquisition or sale of reserve assets can be an autonomous economic activity on their part. Stability in international liquidity where either a rise or decline is desired is not equilibrium, however. Policy actions are required to achieve the shift to the higher or lower level. The need for such policy actions thus may not only come from balance-of-payments developments, but also from developments which are not at all reflected in the balance of payments as already recorded, but which are expected to affect the balance of payments of the future. The recording of changes in international liquidity and the focusing of balance-of-payments analysis on that issue, however, provides the monetary authorities with the information they need for determining whether they are, or are not, moving toward their policy goal.

2. *Measuring Reserves of Monetary Authorities versus Privately Held Foreign-Exchange Assets*

(a) The distinction in statistical practice

If monetary authorities follow the policy of maintaining stable exchange rates they have to distinguish between foreign-exchange assets at their disposal and foreign-exchange assets available to residents of their country but not to the authorities themselves. If balance-of-payments statistics are to serve as a policy guide to the authorities,

18

they must, therefore, be focused on the former. This is generally done in balance-of-payments compilations. Gold holdings of private residents, for instance, are never added to gold holdings of the monetary authorities. Private gold purchases, even from domestic monetary authorities, are always considered to have the same effect on reserves as imports, and in balance-of-payments compilations they are shown either combined with, or next to, imports.

In most countries balance-of-payments statistics are set up in such a way as to draw attention to changes in official reserves. In some countries changes in foreign-exchange assets of private institutions may be added to official reserves, provided these privately held foreign-exchange assets are under relatively effective control by the monetary authorities. Other private purchases or sales of gold and foreign-exchange assets must be considered as part of all other transactions which are the counterpart of shifts in actual or controlled reserve assets of the monetary authorities. Thus the balance of payments does not focus on the changes in international cash assets of all residents of the country—and is in that sense not national in scope. It focuses only on such assets held by a certain section of these residents, the monetary authorities, and in some countries private banks—if they hold liquid assets abroad as part of their cash reserves and if the monetary authorities have the policy tools to obtain these foreign-exchange assets from the banks and are willing and able to exercise these policies even when they conflict with other interests in the economy.

(b)   Theoretical foundations for the existing practices

The distinction between holdings of internationally accepted monetary assets by, or available to, the monetary authorities and those of other residents of the country arises from the obligation of the monetary authorities to maintain the exchange value of the country's currency. Other residents do not have that obligation. Nevertheless, their holdings may have a significance for a country's international liquidity, if they are used as working capital in day-to-day international transactions and thus reduce the turnover in official reserves. Privately held foreign-exchange funds cannot be counted on, however, to meet the need for emergency reserves. They will augment the official reserves only as long as the foreign transactions of a country are more or less in equilibrium and are expected to continue that way.

If conditions change so that international payments exceed receipts, and this change is perhaps expected to persist for some time, private

19

holders of foreign-exchange assets (except where they are under the effective control of the monetary authorities) can be expected to increase their holdings. They will refrain from using their foreign-exchange funds for payments and will tend to meet their foreign-exchange requirements through purchases from the monetary authorities. The latter will have as means to meet the demand for foreign exchange, and thus to defend the exchange value of their currency, only those reserves which they themselves own or effectively control; in most cases they are unlikely to be able to draw on the growing reserves of private residents of their country.

Under such circumstances, the total holdings of international monetary assets may have changed less than the official (and officially controlled) holdings, and for some purposes it may be quite proper to point this out. The changes in total holdings of international monetary assets may enter into the measurement of the change in international liquidity of the country as a whole, but this does not indicate how the liquidity of the monetary authorities has been affected, and whether or not policy actions may be required to safeguard the exchange value of the currency.

3. Private Foreign-Exchange Holdings and Domestic Liquidity

(a) Probable causes of the changes in privately held liquid assets abroad

An increase in privately held foreign-exchange assets may reflect rising requirements for working capital in international funds. If the increase goes further, however, it may indicate a domestic money supply in excess of the need to meet the operating requirements of the economy and a desire to convert the excess supply into international exchange or gold, rather than keeping it in domestic currency units. The conversion may be induced by higher interest rates offered abroad for demand deposits or other liquid investments, or by anticipations of a relative decline in the exchange value of the home currency.

Although a decline in official reserves resulting from an expansion in foreign-exchange holdings by the private sector of the economy should be differentiated from a decline in official reserves resulting from the development of an excess in domestic demand for goods and services over domestic production, in both instances excess monetary liquidity is a necessary condition, and both may reflect rather fundamental changes in the relations between the economy developing the excess demand and the economies of other countries.

20

(b) Excessive domestic liquidity as a common cause of increases in asset-holding and imports

The excess liquidity, of course, can be the result of a rise in the money supply relative to the requirements of the economy, a decline in the demand for cash reserves (resulting in a higher velocity of circulation), or of a shrinkage in the operation of the economy without a corresponding decline in the money supply.

A money supply (or velocity of circulation) rising faster than the domestic capacity to produce may result either in excess liquidity, if prices do not rise sufficiently to equilibrate domestic demand and supply, or in rising prices. In the first case money would flow out of the country both through capital movements—if investment opportunities in the domestic economy are less attractive than those abroad—and through purchases of goods and services—if those produced domestically are less attractive than those produced abroad. If domestic prices of goods and of investments (real or securities) are rising, this indicates that they are more attractive than those available abroad, but as their prices go up their relative attractiveness will decline and the outflow of funds correspondingly increase. A deficit in the balance of payments resulting from rising capital outflows—whether for long-term or shorter-term investments, or from rising net purchases of goods and services—is, therefore, fundamentally due to the same development: an increase in the money supply (or velocity of circulation) relative to the ability of the domestic economy to absorb it. The increase in private domestic holdings of foreign liquid assets is only one form of the general phenomenon.[4] A shrinking output of the domestic economy without a decline in the money supply (or velocity of circulation) reflects a decline in the ability of the economy to attract the current demand.

An outflow of capital for liquid investment abroad may perhaps be viewed with less concern than a net outflow of funds for the purchase of goods and services and longer-term investments, but even a desire to keep liquid funds in other countries may indicate a distrust in one's own currency or banking system, or relatively low marginal earning opportunities for the funds. Such low earning opportunities may reflect

---

[4] It is to be expected that a rise in domestic output will require additional imports of some commodities and services. To avoid a loss of liquidity by the monetary authorities, the rise in domestic demand would have to be accompanied by an increase in the competitive strength of the economy resulting either in offsetting shifts in trade (a rise in exports or a decline in other imports) or in offsetting shifts in capital movements.

merely temporary (perhaps seasonal or cyclical) conditions. If they persist, however, they are likely to reflect a deeper-seated cause for liquidity to be in excess of requirements in the capital-exporting country, and an excess of investment opportunities relative to savings in the capital-importing country, which usually leads to a net outflow of funds on account of other transactions as well.

From the point of view of the strength of the currency, an increase in privately held foreign-exchange reserves can hardly be considered an offset to a decline in reserves held by, or available to, the monetary authorities, unless the latter have effective control over them. In fact, in many historic instances absorption of foreign-exchange resources by private holders caused sufficient losses of foreign-exchange assets to the monetary authorities to impair seriously their ability to defend the currency, making a devaluation of the currency inevitable.

A somewhat related problem can be seen in changes in privately held assets in the form of imported or easily exported commodities. It is conceivable that a country draws on its international reserves to build up such inventories in anticipation of price rises or supply limitations. This, if based on good judgment, may, in fact, save foreign exchange in the long run. A decline in monetary reserves under such circumstances may be considered temporary and not a real loss of liquidity. This interpretation, in effect, combines the changes in monetary reserves with those in "real" reserves. Likewise, a rise in monetary reserves achieved by a reduction in such inventories would not necessarily signify an improvement in the liquidity position of a country. However, the relation of changes in monetary and in "real" reserves is not necessarily temporary. It is conceivable that excess liquidity in the economy can lead to a longer-run build-up of "real" reserves, particularly if prices are expected to rise, affecting monetary reserves in the same way as a prolonged capital outflow.

Whether or not the changes in "real" private reserves should be added to the monetary reserves in evaluating the liquidity position of the monetary authorities will also depend upon their power to force a liquidation of the accumulated inventories and to obtain the foreign exchange thus realized.

A rise in private inventories of imported or exportable goods has often been as important a factor contributing to foreign-exchange difficulties—and devaluations—as private accumulations of monetary assets abroad.

IV. Assets and Liabilities in the Measurement of International Liquidity

1. *Basic General Problems*

As indicated earlier, the principle of balance-of-payments accounting which is based on a necessary equality between total credits and debits does not provide for a separation of those items which may measure changes in the international liquidity of the monetary authorities. That separation is a function of analysis and interpretation of the significance of the various types of transactions.

The first problem arises from the difficulty of determining precisely what constitutes liquidity of the assets as well as the liabilities and finding a borderline which is statistically practicable between liquid and nonliquid assets and liabilities.

A further complication arises from the need to determine what assets are eligible to be included in reserves held by the monetary authorities and over what assets in the hands of private banks, enterprises or persons the authorities have sufficient control to warrant their addition to the official reserves.

Correspondingly, a selection has to be made among the liabilities to be included in the liquidity measurement—that is, whether these ought to consist only of the liabilities of the monetary authorities or also of those of the banking system and other sectors of the economy.

The answer to these questions will depend to a certain extent upon institutional arrangements which may be different in different countries and may change over time. It is futile, therefore, to search for a formula that can be applied to all countries and can be used without change for an indefinite period. Arbitrarily setting up such a formula would in fact lead to an analysis of international transactions that would reflect a preconceived and invariable pattern, rather than an objective appraisal of the prevailing conditions and the problems which they present.

Actually the problem of setting up a measure for liquidity is not limited to the analysis of the balance of international payments but—although perhaps in a less than ideal and uncontroversial way—is solved in the analysis of the financial conditions of corporations and banks. Standards have been devised, perhaps arbitrary at the borders, but nevertheless practicable, by which liquid assets and liabilities are distinguished from others, and relationships are established between liquid assets and liabilities to evaluate the banks' solvency. (The same, of course, applies also to other enterprises.)

Because the dollar serves also as an international medium of exchange, the definition of liquid liability may use criteria similar to those used in the definition of monetary assets in analyzing domestic monetary liquidity and monetary policy. In that connection questions have arisen first, whether to include deposits subject to withdrawal by check, in addition to currency and coins. Later, changing practices in holding reserves made it desirable for certain types of analysis to include in the measure of liquid reserves near-cash assets—such as time deposits, government securities close to maturity, and commercial paper. With changing practices these measures may have to be further adjusted. These difficulties do not preclude, however, the establishment of some rough, but still useful, definition of liquid assets and liabilities.

One could imagine a liquidity measurement in the form of different layers of items—from those most liquid to those less liquid—instead of a single figure. One might further distinguish the degrees to which monetary authorities control foreign-exchange assets held by others, or are potentially affected by liabilities incurred by other sectors of the economy. Such distinctions may be more correct, but also more difficult to use, both for the makers of policies affecting the balance of payments, and for the public.

In a country such as ours, public understanding of balance-of-payments problems is essential because public cooperation and effort are needed to achieve an improvement. The advantages of a more sophisticated and theoretically precise presentation and analysis has to be weighed against the advantages of simplifications which are needed to widen public understanding.

2. Liquidity Measures Appropriate for the United States

(a) Monetary reserves and IMF drawing rights

Gold is currently the most liquid monetary asset and constitutes the ultimate international reserve available for the defense of the dollar. It can be used in all international financial markets to support the exchange value of the dollar or to repurchase from foreign monetary authorities dollars which they have purchased to ensure the proper exchange relationships but which now exceed their requirements.

Convertible foreign currencies which have been acquired by the Treasury since March 1961, and about a year later also by the Federal Reserve System, are also available to support the exchange value of the dollar, but not as freely as gold. In general, a foreign currency acquired by U.S. authorities can be used to support the dollar only if it drops in exchange value against that currency, but it probably could not be sold without permission from the monetary authorities of that country to support the dollar against other currencies. These currencies do not at this time serve as international media of exchange in the same way as the U.S. dollar does, and U.S. holdings of foreign currencies are consequently not quite as liquid as foreign holdings of U.S. dollars.

Drawing rights on the International Monetary Fund may be considered as part of the monetary reserves. Perhaps drawing rights to the extent of the gold-tranche position in the IMF, which are generally granted more or less automatically, may even be included in the liquid reserves. (The gold-tranche position of the United States is measured by the gold subscription to the IMF plus the amount of dollars sold by the IMF to other countries less the purchase of gold or foreign currencies from the IMF.) Inclusion of the gold-tranche position in the IMF in the liquid reserves increases the size of these reserves relative to the size of the outstanding liabilities. Changes in this position does not affect the change in the reserves less liabilities as now measured by the Department of Commerce, and thus does not affect the balance as it is now presented.[1]

A question may be raised whether a liability arising from a drawing

[1] The following examples illustrate this point:

Case I: A foreign country borrows X million dollars from the IMF. This may be recorded in the balance of payments as a decline in U.S. liquid liabilities to the IMF by X million and an increase in U.S. liabilities to the foreign country by the same amount. No change takes place in total U.S. liabilities. Alternatively, if the gold-tranche position in the IMF were included in reserves, this transaction would result in a rise in the position (and consequently in the reserves) by X million, and in a rise in liquid liabilities to the borrowing country also by X million. Again, the rise in assets and liabilities would cancel one another and the change in the net liquidity position would be zero.

Case II: The United States borrows X million dollars from the IMF. Under the first recording procedure this transaction would appear as an increase in liquid liabilities to the IMF offset by a rise in convertible foreign-currency assets by the monetary authorities. Net liquidity would not be changed. The alternative method would show a decline in drawing rights (classified as a reserve asset) which would be offset by larger holdings of foreign currencies. Thus the decline in one type of reserve asset would equal the rise in another type, and the change in net liquidity would also be zero.

on the IMF might not be considered long-term, rather than liquid. In this case, a rise in foreign currency assets held by the monetary authorities would be offset by an increase in long-term or nonliquid liabilities and the balance of payments would appear to have improved. Correspondingly, a repayment to the IMF would appear as a deterioration in the balance of payments. This is one of the borderline cases in which either presentation may be justified.

To measure the extent to which the balance of payments has to be improved, however, the loan should not be considered as part of the solution of the problem. From that point of view, it may be preferable to consider the drawing right as part of the reserve assets, and the actual drawings as merely a change in the composition of the reserves, rather than an increase. In any case, to ensure proper interpretation of the figures, in case this type of transaction is considered to improve the balance of payments, it will be necessary to point specifically to the transaction and to indicate its significance.

(b) Private U.S. holdings of liquid assets abroad

As stated earlier, privately held foreign-currency assets should not be combined with official reserves as a potential support in defense of the exchange value of a currency if they are generally not available to the monetary authorities for that purpose.

The amount of liquid foreign-currency assets held by U.S. banks for their own account is not known. In the statistics on short-term foreign claims reported by banks (published monthly in the *Federal Reserve* and *Treasury Bulletins*), such assets are now combined with those held by the banks in their own name but for the account of their customers, and with those held in the name of the customers but in custody of the banks. Furthermore, the figures combine liquid assets, such as holdings of foreign marketable securities with an early maturity, with trade credits and other receivables. Inquiries have shown, however, that holdings of liquid foreign-currency assets by the banks for their own account are only a very small part of the total of such assets reported by them.

Even the total of foreign-currency assets reported by banks as being held for their own as well as their customers' account in the major foreign financial centers (that is, the major European countries and Canada) in mid-1962 was only about $380 million—or less than 8 percent of the total short-term claims reported by the banks. This amount consisted of about $220 million of deposits in these countries and $160 million of other assets. About half of the deposits were in the United Kingdom, and that amount was about the same as at the end of 1959.

Foreign-currency assets held by nonfinancial concerns in the major foreign financial centers increased in 1960 to about $200 million, but remained at that level thereafter, at least until the middle of 1962. These assets also include liquid funds and various types of credits.

The rather small amount of liquid foreign-currency assets, and particularly deposits, probably indicates that only a relatively small part of U.S. business with foreign countries is conducted in currencies other than U.S. dollars, and that this practice has not changed materially in recent years.

The major part of the foreign-exchange assets held by U.S. residents belong directly or indirectly to nonfinancial business enterprises or individuals. The small holdings by banks for their own account are probably required for their day-to-day business.

In principle, not only liquid bank assets in foreign currencies but also liquid dollar claims against foreign banks could be considered as supplementary to those held by the monetary authorities, provided they are available to the latter. Available statistics do not separate such assets from other claims which banks themselves do not consider cash or near-cash items. Informal inquiries indicate, however, that banks generally do not keep their liquid reserves in foreign assets, not even in short-term loans on the Euro-dollar market. In fact, interest rates on funds placed for relatively short periods in the Euro-dollar market, which may qualify as liquid investments, generally have not been higher than the rates on comparable short-term domestic loans—for instance, to security dealers—or on commercial paper in this country.

U.S. banks keep their secondary reserves entirely in domestic assets such as deposits in other U.S. banks, day-by-day secured loans, or easily marketable securities, for instance government obligations with an early maturity.

If credit is tightened in the United States, the banks will probably attempt to reduce their holdings of foreign assets, but not necessarily faster than those of domestic assets. In fact, since their secondary reserves are in domestic assets, it is likely that they will try to liquidate these first. The effects of credit-tightening policies on foreign assets of U.S. banks, therefore, will be slow since nearly all of these assets consist of loans which can be liquidated only as they mature and the foreign debtors are able to obtain the dollar exchange to repay them.

It must be concluded, therefore, that in the United States privately held assets abroad hardly constitute an effective supplement to the official reserves of the monetary authorities, and should not be combined with the latter in measuring liquidity available for the defense of the dollar.

In case the use of foreign currencies as international media of exchange and as reserve assets increase, U.S. banks may build up their liquid foreign-currency assets above the amounts needed to meet the requirements of current business operations, and use the excess as a part of their secondary cash reserves. If such assets can also be considered to be under effective control of the monetary authorities, the changes in these assets can be included in measuring changes in the international liquidity position of the country's monetary system. There is no evidence so far, however, that such developments have already taken place.

Most of the U.S. dollar assets included by banks in their reports on short-term claims (published monthly in the *Treasury* and *Federal Reserve Bulletins*) are clearly not liquid assets. Of the $5.0 billion of such claims outstanding at the end of December 1962, $3.9 billion—or more than 78 percent—were claims on countries generally not considered financial centers for the placement of funds in liquid assets. The $3.9 billion includes about $1.7 billion of claims on Japan, $1.5 billion of claims on various Latin American countries, the remainder being distributed among other countries, most of which do not have freely convertible currencies.

Many loans classified as short-term are really revolving loans, or drawings on more-or-less long-term lines of credit, to the same customer. Others may be short-term loans to a single customer, but have to be considered long-term claims against the borrower's country, because the country's foreign-exchange resources may not permit it to pay off its short-term debt unless it can borrow on longer terms. Some loans may be set up and classified as short-term to meet balance-sheet requirements of the lending bank, although they are not intended to be called.

Over the postwar period, U.S. statistics on so-called short-term assets abroad have not shown alternate periods of net outflows and inflows of funds but almost only net outflows. In the few periods when reductions in short-term claims were registered in the statistics, they were most often due not to a return flow of capital but to a conversion into long-term loans, mainly by the Export-Import Bank, but sometimes by private sources.

Even the large increase in such claims in 1960 and 1961 did not consist of an outflow of capital for liquid investment abroad, but represented mainly loans to countries other than the financial centers. Of the $1 billion increase in 1960, nearly half was in loans to Japan, and about 20 percent in loans to Latin America and other underdeveloped countries. Contrary to often expressed opinions, the outflow of funds to the financial centers of Europe during that period was only a minor part of the short-term capital outflow reported by banks. Short-term claims on these countries rose in 1960 only by about $150 million, a good part of which were funds reported by the banks on behalf of their customers. Another part consisted of normal commercial and financial loans, rather than funds placed abroad for liquid investment.

Another $150 million of the rise in claims was against Canada, of which a part also represented assets of the banks' customers, and part the usual type of credits.

The change in claims reported for 1961 was quite similar. Except for a very short-term exchange of deposits between a few U.S. banks and foreign banks over the year's end for window-dressing, the increase in total short-term claims reported by banks was also close to $1 billion. Of that amount, about $635 million represented new loans to Japan, about $120 million loans to Latin America, and $135 million loans to other underdeveloped countries. The remainder of the capital outflow was to Canada. Transactions with the major European countries (aside from the special deposit exchange) resulted in small return flows to the United States.

While U.S. banks do not seem to have transferred funds to foreign countries for liquid investment, nonfinancial concerns appear to have increased their short-term assets in Canada and European financial centers by larger amounts in recent years. These assets include trade credits as well as liquid investments. A new questionnaire to get information from nonfinancial enterprises on their liquid investments abroad has recently been circulated, and the preliminary results show that a large part of their assets in Canada consist of time deposits denominated in U.S. dollars. Liquid assets of these enterprises can hardly be considered available to the monetary authorities to defend the exchange value of the dollar, however, and it would be imprudent to consider them as secondary reserves.

(c)   Differences between U.S. and foreign banking practices

Abroad, particularly in some of the major European countries, conditions are different. As long as the dollar is accepted by foreign central banks as part of their official reserves, along with gold, these banks stand ready to buy liquid dollar assets at stated prices. Consequently, in some of these countries, private banks and other private enterprises and persons will be inclined to hold liquid dollars as part of their own reserves, where this is permitted—either in first or second line, depending upon the regulations and customs of the countries concerned. They will hold these dollar assets although their yield is generally a good deal lower than the income they obtain from domestic, but less liquid, investments. Even if small, it may be more than the yield on their legal or other first-line reserves. A credit contraction by foreign central banks will induce private banks and enterprises to sell their dollar assets before they attempt, or are able, to reduce their relatively high-yield domestic assets, and the central-bank reserves will be increased correspondingly.[2]

Because of different institutional arrangements abroad—due partly to the fact that the dollar is a reserve currency and partly to the lack of liquid domestic assets comparable to U.S. Government securities— foreign central banks are in a much better position to augment their reserves from privately held dollar assets than are our monetary authorities to augment their gold holdings by inducing private holders of foreign assets to sell them.

If foreign-exchange assets held by, or at least available to, the monetary authorities are distinguished from those held by private persons or enterprises, it must be recognized that such assets can be transferred not only between monetary authorities themselves, but also between monetary authorities and private holders, and likewise between private holders in the same country and those in different countries. A change in official reserves (and in "controlled" private foreign-exchange assets) in one country, therefore, does not have to be matched by opposite changes in the official reserves of the other countries.

If foreign-exchange assets, including gold, are accumulated by private holders (and such accumulations exceed net purchases of newly mined gold by monetary authorities), the total of all official reserves

---

[2] For instance, German private banks were induced by credit restrictions of the German central bank in the fall of 1959 to reduce their foreign liquid assets, mainly time deposits and market-paper investments, from 4.2 billion DM on October 31, 1959, to less than 2.4 billion DM at the end of December 1960. The subsequent relaxation of restrictions led to an increase of liquid foreign assets to 7.2 billion DM in February 1962. Following that, credit restrictions resulted again in reductions to 5.5 billion DM at the end of June (*Monthly Report of the German Bundesbank*, August 1962, p. 11).

will decline. This may result in defensive policies by the countries losing official reserves, but will not induce expansionary policies by the monetary authorities in the countries whose privately held foreign-exchange assets are increasing.

An increase in private holdings of foreign exchange may, therefore, induce contractive economic policies affecting not only the country originally losing reserves, but other countries as well.[3] This is not different, however, from the effects of hoarding money (or a decline in the velocity of circulation) within the economy of a single country. Indeed, the economy of the world as a whole may be considered to operate similarly to the hypothetical economy of a single country without foreign transactions. To overcome such deflationary tendencies, special measures may have to be considered by the monetary authorities of the different countries.

The distinction between private and public accumulation of foreign-exchange assets may not be as significant with respect to their economic effects as it appears to be. If private recipients of foreign-exchange assets do not want to increase their holdings, but spend them, they will—in general—have to convert the foreign currencies into local currencies. In most countries this will not be possible without selling the foreign-exchange assets to their monetary authorities. In that case, the total of foreign-exchange assets held by all monetary authorities will remain unchanged. It is not certain, however, that the authorities gaining reserves will follow an expansionary policy, offsetting the contractive policies of the authorities losing reserves. If the authorities gaining reserves follow a general policy of increasing their reserve assets, they will hold economic expansion in their country down to a lower rate than their reserve acquisition would otherwise permit. In this case, the foreign-exchange reserves may be considered to have been hoarded—or immobilized by the monetary authorities themselves—and the effect of this policy on the economies of the countries involved will not be much different from the case discussed earlier, where the foreign-exchange receipts were hoarded by private holders.

3. *Liabilities Included in Liquidity Measurement*

Changes in reserves of gold and internationally usable foreign-exchange assets are not the only consideration in the evaluation of the

[3] This problem has been discussed by Poul Host-Madsen in "Asymmetries between Balance of Payments Surpluses and Deficits" in International Monetary Fund *Staff Papers*, Vol. IX, No. 2 (May 1962).

international liquidity position by monetary authorities. Equally important are the country's liabilities which may have to be paid by drawing on the reserves.

(a) The separation of domestic from external liabilities

Banks, in general, attempt to maintain a certain ratio between their reserve assets and their liabilities. The ratio is much larger for demand liabilities than for liabilities requiring notice before they can be withdrawn.

In the case of commercial banks, both domestic and foreign deposits enter into the ratio because both are equally potential claims against the bank's reserves. The same applied also to central banks as long as they had the obligation to defend the exchange value of their country's currency, but within the limits imposed by that obligation, they were also free to maximize their own earnings.

Although several countries have cut the legal and administrative link between banking liabilities and external reserves in order to be able to pursue an independent domestic economic policy, the economic relationship between foreign and domestic transactions has continued. This is particularly the case where international reserves constitute a restraint on policies designed to expand domestic economic activity, unless these policies also succeed in raising the international competitiveness of the economy. The relationship is much less cogent in the case of expanding reserves, which can—for a somewhat longer period at least—be prevented from causing a proportional expansion in the domestic money supply. In many countries where reserves were considered too small to permit domestic business expansion to increase foreign expenditures, attempts were made to cut the relationship between the domestic money supply (which for all practical purposes equals the domestic-banking liabilities) and external reserves through restrictions on the use of foreign exchange and on private purchases of gold. In most countries this attempt to prevent changes in domestic monetary policy from influencing external liquidity did not succeed, however, and changes in the exchange value of their currencies could not be avoided.

In the United States, when, in the early 1930's, the responsibility for maintaining the exchange value of the dollar was transferred to the Treasury, private purchases of monetary gold from the official U.S. gold stock were prohibited. Restrictions on foreign transactions by U.S. residents were not needed, because reserves rose as a result of the depressed level of economic activity here, and because of the inflow of foreign funds for political reasons—including the threat of war in Europe. The fact that the United States, until relatively recently, could pursue a domestic monetary and economic policy without regard to its effect on the international liquidity of the country was due to the coincidence of these developments before the war, the foreign need for U.S. supplies during the reconstruction period, and the ability to draw on the large accumulations of reserves afterwards. These large reserves and the political and economic strength of the United States, which emerged during the first World War and further increased during the second World War, resulted also in the use of the dollar as an international currency and, second only to gold, as a medium for holding international reserves.

These experiences of the United States were the consequence of unique historical developments, but do not disprove the relationship of domestic monetary and economic developments to changes in the external liquidity of a nation. In fact, these relationships have become more evident during the last years even in this country.

While changes in domestic banking liabilities (or in the domestic money supply), relative to the demand for domestically produced goods and services and for reserves of domestic cash assets, can affect the external liquidity of the country, these changes do not enter balance-of-payments compilations until they actually do affect foreign transactions. The fact, however, that data on the excess supply of domestic banking liabilities do not appear in these compilations should not mean that such data do not have to be watched carefully by those responsible for maintaining the exchange value of the country's currency.

Since increases in the excess supply of domestic money may precede the appearance of balance-of-payments difficulties, close observation of the indicators of such developments, followed by appropriate actions may often prevent unfavorable balance-of-payments experiences.

The fact that internal banking liabilities do not appear in balance-of-payments compilations is no reason, however, why changes in external liabilities, particularly liquid liabilities which constitute a direct claim on international reserves, should not be closely watched and, together with the movement in the reserves themselves, serve as a major guide in the formulation of policies designed to maintain the exchange value of the currency.

(b) Reasons for including external liabilities in liquidity measurement

Several more specific reasons for considering changes in external liquid liabilities together with changes in external liquid assets as a measure of changes in external liquidity may be advanced.

(i) An increase in liquid banking liabilities to foreigners constitutes an increase in the supply of domestic currency in the foreign-exchange market, and as such would tend to reduce the exchange value of that currency.

(ii) Even if foreigners are willing to hold additional supplies of a country's currency, or are willing to advance short-term credits to it, it cannot be assumed that foreigners will continue to add to such assets at the same rate and at the same terms for an infinite future. Consequently, the balance on other transactions will have to be changed. The question is only whether the change is to take place when the debt is still small and the debtor country still has the opportunity to make changes which may be constructive in the long run, but take time to accomplish, or whether it has to adjust precipitously, particularly by contracting economic activity or by imposing exchange controls when the creditor countries refuse to extend further credits.

(iii) An increase in indebtedness through liquid or short-term liabilities may make it necessary for the debtor country to offer terms which are increasingly burdensome to itself, in order to compensate the creditors for the rising risk of holding their credits or of extending them further. These terms may not only worsen the balance of payments of the debtor country. They may also impose restrictions on the debtor to conform more closely in his policies to the economic and political doctrines of the creditors.

The higher the liquid debt relative to the liquid assets of the debtor, the more the creditor will be concerned with developments over which the debtor has no immediate control, but which nevertheless are likely to increase the risk for the creditor. Such developments may induce the creditor to convert his claims into gold or other internationally acceptable monetary assets, and thus reduce the reserves of the debtor country. The conversion itself, and its timing, can be most embarrassing to the debtor country, as it will augment the financial difficulties arising from these developments.

(iv) The fact that U.S. banking liabilities and other liquid obligations, such as government or private securities purchased close to maturity, constitute reserve assets for other countries and serve as

34

an international medium of exchange imposes a special responsibility on the United States and, therefore, adds a further reason for paying close attention to the amount of such obligations to foreigners outstanding and its changes.

As indicated earlier, the use of the U.S. dollar for monetary and reserve purposes abroad is based to a large extent upon the unequivocal promise of our monetary authorities to exchange dollars for gold at a fixed price—at least at the request of the monetary authorities of other countries—and the confidence that our monetary authorities will be able and willing to do so in the future. A continued rise in our liquid liabilities relative to the liquid assets held by—or at least available to—our monetary authorities could not help but lead to doubts about the continued ability of our authorities to follow this policy.

Such doubts would affect the foreign policies of official institutions, as well as of banks and other private parties, with respect to holding dollar assets as part of their reserves and, indirectly, accepting dollars in payment of international obligations. It is probably true that, under present conditions, it would be difficult to find another currency that would better meet the requirements for the role as international reserve and international medium of exchange. A decline in confidence in the continued convertibility of the dollar into gold could induce many foreigners—official agencies, as well as private enterprises and persons—to increase the proportion of gold in their reserves. This would not only raise the demand on our gold supply but, by shrinking sharply the international money supply and international reserves, also limit international business in general. Nearly all countries would thus be forced to balance their international receipts and payments more closely through the imposition or extension of controls on foreign transactions.

Even if the use of the dollar as a reserve asset and an international medium of exchange were not dependent upon its tie to gold, but solely upon the recognition of the size and strength of the American economy—which provides a reasonable assurance that foreign holders of dollars can always exchange them for goods, services and financial assets—the amount of liquid dollar assets held abroad could not be permitted to rise without some limitation.

An unlimited rise in the international money supply would have the same effect as a rise in the money supply in a closed economy: to raise prices, cause shifts in purchasing power, incomes, and relative values of assets, and to change incentives to invest and to produce, all of which is likely to have undesirable social and economic repercussions. Furthermore, an excessive rise in the supply of a traditional medium of exchange usually leads to the development of a new type of money which provides a better measure of value and a better means of keeping reserves. In other words, the dollar can continue its function to serve as an international reserve currency, only if its supply held abroad is kept within the limits required to meet monetary and reserve requirements of a growing world economy with a reasonably stable price level. This responsibility imposes upon us the need to keep our foreign transactions over a longer period, perhaps the length of a business cycle, in an appropriate balance, whether or not the dollar is directly tied to gold.

The use of the dollar as an international medium of exchange requires that transfers of liquid dollar assets by this country to or from foreigners be considered together with gold in the balance-of-payments compilations, if it is intended to measure the net movement of monetary assets between this and other countries and to separate these monetary movements from other foreign transactions.

With the major exceptions of the British pound and the French franc, foreign currencies are not generally used as an international medium of exchange and reserve asset—and even these currencies are used for such purposes mainly in their own currency areas. Except for transactions within the sterling and French-franc areas, international payments of other countries are made mainly in dollars and gold, and consequently result in a decline in their monetary assets rather than in an increase in their liquid liabilities. The use of the dollar as a means of settling balances between the monetary authorities of other countries goes back before World War II and is related to the use of the dollar as an official reserve asset. During more recent years, however, as the dollar supply abroad has become more plentiful and restrictions on the use of dollars have been lifted in most of the European countries, the dollar has been used increasingly also as a medium of exchange in private transactions.

If it is intended to measure for a foreign country changes in the net international liquidity position not only of its monetary authorities but of all of its residents, the total net movements of gold and liquid dollar assets will have to be considered.

Residents of the United States—even more than those of other countries—transact their international business primarily in dollars. Dollar transactions, however, do not appear in balance-of-payments compilations as changes in this country's holdings of monetary assets (as is the case in other countries), but as changes in its liquid liabilities.

Since private residents of the United States generally do not need liquid assets in foreign currencies and actually hold only relatively small amounts, and no information is available on their holdings of monetary gold, the net changes in the international liquidity position of the monetary authorities of the United States and in that of all residents (including the authorities) are for all practical purposes usually not far apart. In this respect the U.S. balance of payments differs, therefore, from those of other countries.

4. Further Problems of Measuring International Liquidity

(a) General remarks

Although it is reasonable to include liquid liabilities to foreigners as well as liquid assets of our monetary authorities in the measure of the net liquidity position available for the defense of the exchange value of the dollar, the next question is concerned with the selection of those items which may be considered in that measure.

Combination of changes in the holdings of gold and convertible currencies by the monetary authorities and of liquid liabilities into a single figure has the advantage of providing a focus for balance-of-payments analysis, which is relatively easily understood and permits comparisons of changes between periods, but which in many respects also has weaknesses.

A change in net liquidity consisting of a change in monetary assets may be considered more significant and to require more urgent attention than a change in liabilities. While liquid liabilities are a potential claim on our reserves, and while the dollar supply abroad tends to affect the exchange value of the dollar, a rise in liabilities essentially serves as a warning that the reserves may be endangered unless the pattern of foreign transactions is changed. It is not yet equivalent, however, to a decline of the reserves. Equally, a decline in reserves matched by decline in liquid liabilities is a more unfavorable development than a zero change in the composite balance would suggest. Conversely, a rise in reserves, offset by a rise in liabilities, is perhaps a more favorable change, particularly if the liabilities exceed the gold and convertible-currency reserve.

A complete analysis of the balance of payments should, therefore, draw attention to changes in the asset as well as the liability components of the net liquidity position.

The problem of selecting the liabilities which may be viewed as a potential claim against the reserve assets may be divided into two parts, the first being concerned with the foreign holders of dollar assets, the other with the type of asset which may be classified as liquid.

(b) Types of foreign creditors

Only foreign monetary authorities may purchase gold from U.S. monetary authorities to meet monetary purposes, including the accumulation of official reserves. This does not preclude, however, that, indirectly, dollars held by other foreigners may also be used to buy gold here. To stabilize the gold value of the dollar and to dispel speculative notions that the present gold policy of the United States might be changed, gold has also been sold by the Bank of England on the London gold market to private buyers for dollars, which were then used by the Bank of England to repurchase the gold from the United States. Furthermore, privately held dollars abroad can be sold to foreign monetary authorities, which can use them to purchase gold here.

In fact, dollars held by private foreign holders may represent a greater risk of a drain on our gold supply than dollars held by certain central banks. Private holders may exchange their dollars for speculative reasons into currencies of countries, such as Switzerland, which customarily keep their reserves in gold, while central banks of some of the major countries, such as Germany or Japan, which keep a large part of their reserves in dollars, are much less likely to be motivated by fears or speculative reasons to convert their dollar assets into gold.

Also, as has already been pointed out, foreign monetary authorities have considerable power to obtain dollar assets from their commercial banks; some of the dollar holdings in Germany, for instance, are held by the commercial banks under repurchase agreements with the German Bundesbank, and similar arrangements have also been made between the central bank and commercial banks in Italy.

The distinction between holdings of central banks and private banks is therefore not quite realistic. If it is held desirable to consider changes in liquid liabilities together with those of monetary reserves as a measure of changes in our international-liquidity position, it is quite unrealistic to limit the liabilities to those held by monetary authorities.[4]

[4] The proposition to include only liabilities to foreign monetary authorities in the measurement of the balance on foreign transactions was made by Poul Host-Madsen in "Asymmetries between Payments Surpluses and Deficits" *op.cit.*, pp. 190ff, and in "Measurements of Imbalances in World Payments." International Monetary Fund *Staff Papers*, Vol. IX, No. 3 (November 1962), p. 351.

The measurement recommended there would include in the balance changes

Furthermore, if the latter were done, a shift of dollar assets between foreign private banks and their central banks, because of policy actions of these central banks to meet domestic economic objectives, would be interpreted as a change in the U.S. balance of payments. The same would be the case if dollar payments were made between two foreign countries, in one of which the dollars were held by private banks or persons, while in the other foreign-exchange holdings were concentrated in the central banks.

Even statistically it is not possible to determine from U.S. banking data how much of the dollar liabilities ultimately represent dollar holdings of foreign monetary authorities. Many of the latter hold their dollars in foreign branches of American banks or in foreign banks which can pay higher interest rates than can be obtained here on deposits or government bills. This they can do because they are not subject to the same stringent reserve requirements and other restrictions as domestic banks have to observe. These branches or foreign banks in turn hold their dollars here in the United States, or lend them to other foreigners whose dollar obligations are more or less covered by dollar assets. In U.S. statistics these dollars appear as liabilities to the foreign private banks which are the immediate holders. The extent to which foreign official dollar reserves are held here through private banks is not known.

From tabulations in *International Financial Statistics* (published

---

in liabilities to foreign monetary authorities, regardless of whether they are liabilities of domestic monetary authorities or of the domestic private sector. In other words, a deposit in a private bank is considered a monetary liability if it is held by a foreign central bank, and changes in such deposits are considered monetary transactions, while the same kind of deposits acquired by foreign private banks or other foreign residents are not. Conversely, a deposit held in a private bank by a foreign private bank or other private resident becomes an investment, while the same kind of deposit held by a foreign central bank is a monetary claim against the monetary reserves of the debtor country. No distinction in this respect is made between countries whose currencies serve as international money and those whose currencies are used essentially only in domestic transactions.

This treatment distinguishes movements of monetary assets and liabilities from those of other assets and liabilities, not on the basis of whether a country's domestic debtors are private or official, but whether the foreign claimants are private or official.

No parallel recommendation is made with respect to assets. If the principles recommended for liabilities were extended to assets, a private loan to a foreign monetary authority would have to be treated as a monetary transaction raising the reserve assets of the creditor country and reducing the net reserves of the debtor country. A private loan to other foreigners involving precisely the same terms would be considered a nonmonetary transaction with an entirely different effect on the balance on international transactions of the lending country.

monthly by the International Monetary Fund) in which it is attempted to reconcile foreign-exchange assets and liabilities of official organizations and banks, principally in dollars and sterling, it appears that foreign official dollar reserves held here through private banks around the middle of 1962 may easily have exceeded $2 billion.[5] The rise in such indirect holdings occurred primarily in 1960. In the second half of 1962 some shift back to direct official holdings may have taken place.

(c)   Types of liabilities

Short-term liabilities reported by U.S. banks consist almost entirely of foreign deposits in these banks, and marketable liquid securities, such as Treasury bills and bankers' acceptances.[6] In addition, foreign holdings of government securities with an original maturity of over one year should also be considered as liquid liabilities. Most of these securities are, in fact, held by foreign official institutions and international organizations as part of their reserves, and are usually purchased a relatively short time before they mature. They are for all practical purposes as liquid an investment as short-term bills. A small part of these securities are, however, held by private investors for longer-term investments, but existing statistics do not permit a separation of their purchases and sales. Although the inclusion of their holdings with other liquid liabilities may be in error, this error is much smaller than if all transactions in such government securities were considered long-term capital movements.

A separate case, also difficult to classify, is nonmarketable government securities. Several types may be distinguished. Some are non-

[5] Oscar L. Altman (in "Recent Developments in Foreign Markets for Dollars and Other Currencies," published in *Factors Affecting the United States Balance of Payments* by the Joint Economic Committee, 87th Congress, 2d Session [Government Printing Office, Washington, 1962], pp. 483-523) estimates that U.S. dollars constituted about 85 percent of the foreign-currency markets in Europe, which he "guessed" to amount to about $4-5 billion by the middle of 1962. He indicates that "at least two-thirds of the funds came directly or indirectly from central banks and monetary authorities" (p. 517) and that "a large proportion of the dollars dealt with in foreign markets, but a modest proportion of the other currencies, is directly or indirectly owned by central banks and other monetary authorities" (p. 490). On the basis of these figures it would appear that at least $2.5 billion of foreign official funds were held in private banks and consequently reported in U.S. statistics as liabilities to private parties. This is nearly half of the $5.4 billion of short-term liabilities to foreign private banks reported by U.S. banks for June 30, 1962.

[6] This composition of foreign short-term liabilities by U.S. banks is entirely different from that of their foreign short-term assets, although both assets and liabilities are labeled "short-term." The difference becomes evident only through an examination of the subdivisions, and further investigations of the principal contents of each of these subgroups.

interest-bearing notes given to, and held by, certain international organizations as part of the U.S. capital subscription. These notes are payable in freely transferable dollar funds. Transfers of such notes to these organizations obviously creates a liability for the United States, but does not constitute a transfer of freely disposable monetary assets. In 1962, holdings of these notes by all international organizations except the IMF were shifted from liquid to nonliquid liabilities and prior years' figures were correspondingly revised. This was done in the statistics on short-term liabilities published in the *Treasury* and *Federal Reserve Bulletins* as well as in the Balance-of-Payments compilations of the Department of Commerce.

Another case is nonmarketable, but interest-bearing obligations sold abroad by the Treasury or the Federal Reserve Banks. Some of these obligations are payable within a few weeks or months, some have a longer maturity period, but among the latter some are convertible at a few days' notice. Some are foreign-currency obligations, and others are payable in dollars. Some may be held by the foreign monetary authorities as part of their reserves and others are not counted into foreign reserves. It would be difficult to devise a classification which would clearly distinguish the degrees of liquidity of these obligations. Furthermore, it would be difficult to judge to what extent sales or repurchases of such obligations constitute basic changes in this country's distance from an equilibrium in its international transactions, and thus provide a substitute for changes in other transactions through which a new equilibrium would have to be achieved. There is no question that such obligations themselves cannot be used to purchase gold. There still remains a question, however, how much these securities, particularly those which are convertible on short notice, differ in the way they are used by foreign central banks which buy them from regular securities, and how the purchases of these special U.S. government obligations affect the desire of the purchasing central banks to hold additional amounts of liquid dollar assets, or to convert new dollar receipts into gold. Experience with these transactions is too recent to answer these questions, if, indeed, an answer is possible at all. A reasonable way to set the line of demarcation between liquid and other liabilities would be to classify those obligations as liquid which mature or are convertible into free cash at the option of the buyer and with relatively little delay.

Short-term liabilities to foreigners reported by nonfinancial concerns may be considered a borderline category, but it seems preferable not to include them among liquid liabilities for the purpose of balance-of-payments analysis. The precise nature of these liabilities is not known, but they are not likely to be marketable obligations. (If foreigners hold such obligations and they are placed in the custody of banks, they are included in the liabilities reported by the banks.) A large part of the liabilities reported by nonfinancial concerns apparently arise from advance payments by foreigners on purchase contracts, which will be extinguished by the delivery of the goods ordered rather than by payment of cash. A question may arise, however, if such liabilities are incurred by postponing payments for imports or other current obligations. Although the rise in such liabilities does not arise from the transfer of a money instrument (for example, a check drawn against a U.S. bank), it does reflect a condition which is unstable in the longer run, and requires an adjustment in international transactions. If the rise in such liabilities is not counted as part of the balance, it should at least be shown in the balance-of-payments presentation in such a way that its significance can easily be noticed.

The figures for liquid liabilities do not include foreign purchases and sales of corporate or local government bonds purchased shortly before their maturity, although such investments can be as liquid as those in other securities with an early maturity. Such purchases and sales cannot be separated from those of other transactions in bonds, and in this case the errors are probably minimized by considering all these transactions as changes in nonliquid investments by foreigners.

(d)   Ties between short-term assets and liquid liabilities

This measure of net liquidity as used here is sometimes criticized on the ground that it does not include liquid private assets but does take into consideration liquid private liabilities. The reasons for doing so have already been explained.

Liquid foreign assets held by banks are very small, they are used for current business operations and not as reserves, and consequently are not available to the monetary authorities. Even if they were, the effect of a combination of these balances with the official reserves would be very small. The somewhat more important liquid foreign assets of nonfinancial enterprises are not likely to be available for the defense of the exchange value of the dollar and combining them with the official reserves would clearly be misleading.

There are instances, however, when adjustments in the measurement of changes of the liquidity position may be desirable. This would be the case when private assets and private liabilities are closely tied, so that foreign claims can only be exercised against these assets and not against gold. The exchange of deposits between U.S. and foreign banks over the year-end of 1961 may be an example. If precise data on such exchanges were available the liabilities could be considered non-liquid, or the assets and liabilities arising from these transactions could be netted out, and the transactions, in effect, eliminated from the balance of payments. In either case, the figures measuring the decline in net liquidity would have been about $100 million less in 1961, but an equal amount higher in the following year.

Another case that might justify adjustments in the measurement of the net liquidity position would involve foreign funds earmarked here against letters of credit or as compensating balances against loans.

As financial stringencies, particularly in Europe and Japan, have decreased in recent years, the use of letters of credit in trade has probably declined, but with the rise in bank credits more funds have been set aside as compensating balances. No information on earmarked funds is available, but with the principal reasons for earmarking moving in opposite directions, the total may not have changed as much as the rise in compensating balances alone. Compensating balances vary between loans and between lending banks, but are reported to be generally between 10 and 20 percent of the loan. With loans, including acceptance credits, increasing about $640 million in 1960 and about $890 million in 1961, the increase in earmarked liabilities would have been about $100 million in 1960 and about $135 million in 1961. Even a correction in the change in the net liquidity position of the United States in these years ($3.9 and $2.4 billion, respectively) by the full amount of the estimated rise in compensating balances, without counting the possible decline in funds earmarked against letters of credit, would not have altered the analysis of the U.S. balance of payments significantly.

Another instance that is sometimes cited, in which changes in the net liquidity position appear to be overstated, occurs when deposits in U.S. dollars are made in foreign banks, which, in turn, redeposit these dollars in the United States.[7] The same applies to any loan in U.S. dollars to foreigners who redeposit the dollars here, sometimes for limited periods until they can use the funds.

Deposits in U.S. dollars by American enterprises or persons are

[7] See Oscar L. Altman: "Canadian Markets for U.S. Dollars" published in *Factors Affecting the U.S. Balance of Payments*, Joint Economic Committee, 87th Congress, 2d Session (Government Printing Office, Washington, 1962), pp. 536f.

made frequently in Canadian banks because of higher interest rates offered, or, prior to 1963, because of tax advantages. (A U.S. corporation was able to combine the Canadian tax on these interest earnings, which is lower than the U.S. corporate income tax, with the tax on the distributed corporate earnings of its subsidiaries, which is higher than the U.S. corporate income tax, so as to be able to derive full benefit from tax credits against U.S. corporate-income-tax obligations.)

U.S. dollar deposits can, of course, also be made in other countries. If these funds are rerouted back to the United States by foreign banks through their U.S. agencies, the question is justified whether this type of transaction is not essentially domestic, as the funds are deposited abroad only *pro forma*, because the U.S. agencies are by U.S. regulation not permitted to accept deposits directly.

The case is not as simple as it appears, however. The funds deposited abroad are transferred to foreign organizations and under their control. The question is whether these organizations have to keep the equivalent amount in claims on the United States so long as they have the U.S.-dollar liabilities represented by the original deposits. If that is the case, U.S. private assets should indeed be netted out against the liabilities arising from the reinvestment of these funds by the foreign banks in the United States. This does not have to be the case, however. These dollar funds, particularly if they are derived from longer-term time deposits, could be sold by the foreign banks for local currency, so long as the foreign banks cover their obligation in U.S. dollars through forward contracts. Such sales could lead to a gold outflow. Or the foreign bank could make dollar loans to residents of its own or of other foreign countries, who, in turn, could convert the dollars into the currencies of their countries. A considerable part of the dollars deposited in Canada are invested by the Canadian banks in the Euro-dollar market, and some of these funds may be borrowed by organizations which need local-currency funds and consequently sell the borrowed dollars.[8]

U.S.-dollar loans are reported to have been made by Canadian banks to subsidiaries of U.S. corporations in substitution of capital outflows through direct investments. At least in one instance a subsidiary has re-lent the money to its parent company. In this case, the short-term private dollar outflow was offset in the balance of payments by a capital inflow through a direct-investment transaction, as the loan by the foreign subsidiary to its U.S. parent company was recorded in the

[8] Oscar L. Altman, *op.cit.*, p. 534.

intercompany account. Thus, no change was recorded in accounts entering into the computation of the liquidity position of the United States.

If data were available, a case might be made for netting out those liquid liabilities reported by agencies of foreign banks, which they have to hold against deposit obligations of their parent companies to U.S. residents. It is not likely, however, that such data can be developed, since these foreign banks also receive deposits in U.S. dollars from residents of their own and of third countries, and it is not possible to link each of the various investments of these funds with the different nationalities of the banks' depositors.

A perfect statistical solution to this problem may therefore not be possible. Further information might help to decide, however, which procedure for treating such transactions would result in lesser errors, that which is based on the assumption that the entire amount of these liabilities is a part of the liquid dollar supply held by foreigners, or that which assures that the major part of the assets abroad are offset against private dollar liabilities.

(e) Autonomous changes in foreign demand for liquid dollar assets

The use of the dollar as an international medium of exchange and as an international reserve asset raises the question whether an increase in international transactions by the rest of the world would not require an increase in foreign dollar holdings. In that case, it may perhaps be assumed that foreign countries will pursue an active policy to increase their assets, and this increase may be considered a long-term, possibly even permanent, liability of the United States. If this argument is accepted, the changes in net liquidity of the United States in each accounting period will have to be adjusted by an amount corresponding to the increase during that period in foreign requirements for dollar holdings.

In principle, the argument appears to be correct. It is difficult, however, to measure the need for additional dollar reserves of foreign countries. Official reserves are needed by foreign countries to meet excesses of foreign-exchange requirements over foreign-exchange receipts. These excesses may, but do not necessarily have to, rise in proportion to the total value of international business.[9] Excesses can

---

[9] This is essentially Triffin's assumption with respect to the need for an expanded amount of world reserves, in Robert Triffin, *Gold and the Dollar Crisis* (Yale University Press, 1960), Chapter 4. The validity of this assumption was disputed by Oscar L. Altman in *The Dollar in Crisis*, edited by Seymour E. Harris (Harcourt, Brace and World, Inc., New York and Burlingame, 1961), pp. 256ff.

arise from seasonal, cyclical, and other developments, both economic and political. Even if the total turnover does not rise, the need for reserves may change, and if the turnover rises, other developments, including international cooperation to mitigate cyclical fluctuations, provide international credit facilities, and counteract speculative capital movements may stabilize, or even reduce, reserve requirements. Requirements for an increased amount of the medium of exchange to facilitate the higher volume of business transactions may be offset by a more intensive use, or a higher velocity, of the amount currently available. The development of the Euro-dollar market appears to have had this effect. Holding of dollar assets as liquid reserves by foreign banks also depend upon the availability of liquid investment opportunities within their own countries—that is, the development of marketable short-term debt instruments by their governments and major enterprises.

The amount of liquid dollar assets required abroad as a consequence of the use of the dollar as an international-reserve currency is subject to change, therefore, and it would be difficult to devise a method by which changes in that amount could be estimated periodically for inclusion in balance-of-payments compilations. This does not mean, however, that the problem does not have to be kept in mind by those responsible for policies affecting the balance of payments, even if it cannot be evaluated in quantitative terms.

The fact that the dollar is used as an international medium of exchange and that dollars consequently are needed as working capital to make payments in the United States as well as abroad is sometimes used as an argument that not all of the liabilities can be considered claims against U.S. monetary reserves, and that consequently the U.S. liquidity position is much stronger than the ratio of liquid liabilities to reserves may indicate.

The argument overlooks, however, that the balance of payments does not measure the liquidity position itself, but its changes, and that the changes in foreign dollar holdings do not necessarily have to correspond to the changes in foreign requirements for dollars as a circulating medium.

Secondly, the use of the dollar as an international medium of exchange and as a reserve asset for foreign countries cannot be taken for granted, even if the international transactions of the United States comprise a large part of worldwide international business operations. In order to conduct their business with the United States, which in recent years may have amounted to as much as $60 billion counting both receipts and payments, foreign countries would require about $2 billion in demand deposits here. This calculation is based on the assumption that the turnover in their funds would approximately equal the turnover of domestic demand deposits.[10] The actual holdings of liquid dollar assets by foreign countries at the end of 1961 were more than ten times that amount.

The role of the dollar in the current system of international payments is based essentially on confidence in its unrestricted use and its full exchangeability into gold. An increase in the supply of liquid dollar assets held by foreign countries relative to the reserves held by U.S. monetary authorities might ultimately impair that confidence. In this case, not only the increment in their dollar holdings would be in excess of foreign requirements and perhaps exchanged for gold, but foreign countries might even attempt to reduce their holdings below the levels previously held. Even transactions with the United States would not necessarily have to be conducted in dollars. If confidence in the dollar were impaired abroad, foreign countries could require payments in other currencies and U.S. residents would accept other currencies from them. Many countries participate in international transactions, but that does not require that their transactions have to be conducted in their own currencies, or that such currencies have to be held by other countries as working capital. The use of the dollar as working capital in international transactions is not an absolute necessity. It is not the use of the dollar for such purposes that creates the foreign demand for it as a reserve asset, but rather its acceptability as a reserve asset gives the dollar the status to be used as a medium of exchange and for working-capital purposes.

Even if there is an increase in the foreign demand for liquid dollar assets, the rise in U.S. liquid liabilities relative to liquid reserves increases the financial exposure of the United States to changes in confidence in the dollar arising from economic and political developments inside and outside the United States and imposes the need for restraints in our own policy.[11] The problem is, therefore, whether a rise in the foreign demand for increased reserves should not be met by other means, several of which have been proposed and discussed.[12]

[10] In 1961 debits to demand deposits in nonfinancial centers were 26.1 times the average outstanding, in the six major centers other than New York and Chicago 36.8 times, and in the two major centers 70.0 times.

[11] This point is also emphasized by Triffin.

[12] For instance by George N. Halm: "Special Problems of a Key Currency in Balance of Payments Deficit" in *Factors Affecting the United States Balance of Payments, op.cit.*, pp. 554ff.

V. Balance-of-Payments Equilibrium: Conceptual Problems and Alternative Measurements

1. *Temporary versus Longer-run Changes in Net Liquidity Position*

Although net changes in international liquidity relevant to the defense of the exchange value of the currency may be the primary focus of balance-of-payments analysis, it is not sufficient merely to show these changes and the transactions with which they have been associated. A major purpose of the analysis is, in fact, to distinguish those changes which seem to be of relatively short duration from those which are likely to reflect a longer-run trend.

What is short or long run in this connection is not simply a time question, however. If balance-of-payments analysis is to serve as a guide to monetary authorities, it must distinguish between those developments which can be expected to reverse themselves without the need for policy actions and those which require a change in policies to restore an equilibrium. Whether or not, in case of a decline in net liquidity, policy changes are indicated, depends not only upon the developments themselves, but upon the size of the reserves or external credit available for temporary use relative to the cumulative effects of these developments on net liquidity. The cumulative effects are not only a function of time, but also of the intensity of the changes in net liquidity. A country short of reserves and borrowing facilities may have to take defensive actions, while another country with a higher net liquidity could, under the same conditions, wait until the situation resulting in the initial decline in net liquidity reverses itself.

Downward changes in net liquidity usually present a more acute problem than do upward changes for those responsible for policies affecting the balance of payments. While longer-run improvements in net liquidity can also create problems, their correction is usually less urgent and can be more easily entrusted to the economic forces which such developments themselves set in motion. In some instances, monetary authorities have made it a matter of policy to prevent these forces from operating when it was assumed that improvement in liquidity was merely temporary—or that the corrective forces might grow into inflationary developments, which would check and eventually reverse the rise in external liquidity, while the inflation itself might become increasingly difficult to control.

Temporary changes in the net liquidity position may be the result of seasonal or cyclical fluctuations. Seasonal fluctuations can be reasonably well recognized. This is not equally true of cyclical movements, however, and to evaluate their potential cumulative effect on the net liquidity position in relation to the available reserves and credit facilities is more hazardous. The provision of adequate credit facilities through the International Monetary Fund or through international agreements continues to be one of the major tasks of the international community, to enable countries to withstand losses in net liquidity due to declining business activity of their trading partners or to greater growth in their own than in the business activity of their trading partners.

In addition to seasonal and cyclical changes, specific transactions or types of transactions may have to be distinguished. Some transactions may be relatively large, but either not recurring at all or only for a limited period of time; others can be expected to be reversed before their cumulative effect is large enough to require policy actions; in still other cases, the reversal may perhaps require policy actions, but of a type which can be easily taken and which can be counted on to have the desired result.

It is important to separate transactions having a temporary influence on the net liquidity position from the other transactions, and to indicate what the changes in the net liquidity position would have been as a result of the more enduring transactions or conditions. Care must be taken, however, that any special transactions or conditions whose effect can be strong enough to require policy actions are either not included in that adjustment of the change in net liquidity, or at least shown separately from the more recurrent types of transactions and clearly labeled.

What transactions or conditions may be separated out as having only a temporary effect on the net liquidity position and, consequently, what may be considered to be the more "basic" balance during any one period, or what may be the change in that more basic balance is, as has been indicated, determined by economic analysis. Analysis has to be adapted to changing conditions as they affect the transactions themselves, and also as they affect the standard by which changes in the balance on these transactions are measured. As net liquidity or credit facilities increase, more transactions can be included in the category whose changes are likely to be automatically reversed—and can therefore more or less be ignored in the formulation of policies to defend the exchange value of the currency—than will be the case when net liquidity is low and credit facilities are relatively restricted.

It is also possible that transactions between countries essentially equal in competitiveness and following similar monetary policies may change rather quickly, while the same transactions between countries which are unequal in these respects show a much greater persistence in their effect on the net liquidity positions of the countries concerned.

Another problem to be considered has to do with the relationships between the different types of transactions: a transaction of temporary significance need not necessarily have an effect on the liquidity position, but may be offset during the accounting period by another transaction. An example of this might be a large conversion of, say, a short-term loan into a long-term loan or investment, or a large export financed by a loan. The precise interrelationship of transactions cannot always be fully evaluated, however.

It would be fallacious, therefore, to assume that one or another type of transaction always belongs in a category which can be designated as basic, while others do not.[1] There is no short-cut in careful analysis and no easy substitute for it.

Among U.S. transactions in recent years, which have been both outstandingly large and not likely to continue in that magnitude, were for instance, the large purchases of petroleum concessions in Venezuela in 1956 and 1957, or the purchase of minority interests in its British subsidiary by Ford at the end of 1960. These transactions resulted in dollar transfers to the countries in which the investments were made. There is no question that in a quarter-to-quarter analysis they were responsible for equivalent and relatively large shifts in the balance, as measured by the change in the net liquidity position. Whether the changes in year-to-year comparisons also were significant is a matter of further analysis. As the time period is increased, the effect of these special transactions relative to all other transactions is, of course, reduced, and the possibility is increased that the international money flow will be reversed by other transactions which the special trans-

[1] See also the following discussion of the distinction of "basic" transactions from those "sensitive to monetary policies," proposed by Hal B. Lary in *Problems of the United States as a World Trader and Banker* (Princeton: Princeton University Press for the National Bureau of Economic Research, 1963).

actions induce. A large dollar outflow to a nearby country (for example, through a loan) may result—after some lapse of time—in a rise of exports to that country reversing a large part of the dollar outflow, so that the net effect on the liquidity position for the longer period will be considerably less than during the period in which the loan was made.

Other transactions which may be considered as special or of only temporary significance are, for instance, such large loans as the $250 million loan to the United Kingdom at the end of 1957 to assist in the defense of the British pound, or the failure of the United Kingdom, for the same reason, to pay the installment on its 1946 loan.

The large advance debt repayments by foreign countries occurring in 1959, 1961, and 1962 may also be considered special transactions. Although such transactions have occurred several times in the last few years and more may take place in the near future, they caused substantial quarter-to-quarter fluctuations in changes in net liquidity position. In order to see the more enduring trends in the balance of payments, it is helpful to analyze changes in the liquidity position as if these transactions had not taken place. The advance debt repayments may also be considered as temporarily helpful transactions, which cannot be sustained over a very long period of time, because the debt of countries in a position to repay ahead of schedule is relatively limited. Thus, these repayments may also be looked upon as drawings on limited reserves—and it would be desirable not to show these transactions in the balance.

Another type of transaction which cannot be expected to be sustained over a long period of time is large loans either to private U.S. enterprises or to the U.S. Government. The borrowers may not intend to repeat such transactions frequently, or the creditor countries may not have the financial facilities or the desire to make such loans continuously. Except in emergencies, increases in foreign indebtedness, even if they affect the liquidity of the country during the same period favorably, may not be considered a desirable long-run way of balancing other transactions—unless the loans are connected with the financing of operations to strengthen the international competitiveness of the economy sufficiently to obtain at least the means with which to service and repay the loans.

Changes in transactions, which may have a temporary effect, include those which are caused by conditions at home or abroad which affect production or transportation, such as strikes, exceptional harvests, the weather. Political developments at home or abroad may temporarily influence transactions in goods and services, as well as financial transactions. Some of the political developments may have longer-run effects, and it may not be easy to distinguish these from others which are likely to be reversed within relatively short periods.

Another example of a relatively temporary development which had repercussions in many different types of transactions was the Canadian exchange crisis in 1962. The extent of its reserve losses during the first half of the year made it inevitable that Canada should have to take action to stop these losses. The repercussions of the Canadian reserve losses on the U.S. balance of payments could be considered a temporary development, therefore, and an analysis of the longer-run trends in the U.S. balance of payments required an estimate of the effects of these developments. Some of these effects may have appeared in an acceleration of exports; some in larger distributions of dividends by Canadian subsidiaries to their U.S. parent companies; some in lower outflows of capital through direct investments, new issues of Canadian bonds in the U.S. market, or other loans. Some of the capital inflows to the United States from Canada probably were not recorded and thus tended to reduce net debits or increase net credits in "Errors and Omissions." The effects of the Canadian exchange crisis on the U.S. balance of payments during that period cannot be determined, however, by an analysis of each of the various types of transactions. Many of the changes within these transactions probably did not affect the cash flow, but were offset in other items. The analysis may be somewhat more fruitful, although still subject to many uncertainties, if the aggregate of all transactions with Canada (excluding gold movements and changes in liquid U.S. liabilities) is compared with that of a previous period, and changes in this aggregate compared with changes in Canadian reserves over the same period.

A similar analysis was required for the subsequent periods when Canadian reserves increased again. The corresponding deterioration of the U.S. balance of payments may also be considered a temporary development and a balance estimated by abstracting from it. The estimate of what should be considered temporary in this phase of the development is much more difficult to determine than for the period when Canadian reserves dropped, because the limits to the rise are much less definite than those to the decline. The rise can go considerably further than necessary for a mere recovery of reserves. Con-

52

sequently, the corresponding deterioration in the U.S. balance of payments cannot be considered temporary with the same degree of certainty as the preceding improvement was, and the uncertainty in finding a balance reflecting longer-run trends is correspondingly increased.

2. Singling Out Volatile Capital Movements

(a) Short-term capital flows

Various attempts have been made to set up a balance on all transactions other than short-term capital movements and "Errors and Omissions" (on the ground that changes in "Errors and Omissions" also reflect mainly shifts in short-term capital movements) as a measurement of the more fundamental trends in the balance of payments as distinguished from more volatile shifts of capital.[2] Walter R. Gardner would also include in the more volatile types of capital movements transactions in outstanding securities, new issues of securities, and redemptions.[3] The latter are combined in a subtotal designated as "Open Market Capital."

Many analysts believe that transactions included in the statistics under the heading of short-term capital flows are primarily shifts of cash balances into other currencies, either to escape uncertainty from risks of restrictions on the use of the funds or of currency devaluations or to take advantage of anticipated appreciations, or of temporarily higher earning opportunities.[4] These analysts assume that cash hold-

[2] Hal B. Lary, op.cit., pp. 137ff.

[3] Walter R. Gardner: "An Exchange Market Analysis of the U.S. Balance of Payments," International Monetary Fund Staff Papers (May 1961), p. 198.

[4] Ragnar Nurkse writes in "Conditions of International Monetary Equilibrium," quoted from Readings in the Theory of International Trade, op.cit., pp. 7, 8:

Another item [in addition to a net change in a country's international currency reserve] that should be excluded [from the rest of the transactions in order to measure a disequilibrium in the foreign transactions of a country] is short-term capital movements. Such capital transactions may be of two kinds. They may be of the equilibrating kind, such as used to occur in the gold standard mechanism in response to temporary changes in discount rates or to movements in exchange rates within the gold points. In that case they merely take the place of—and fulfill the same function as—transfers of gold or foreign exchange reserves. A country with a deficit in its balance of payments can cover the deficit either by an outflow of gold or an inflow of foreign short-term funds, if it is able to attract such funds by raising its bank rate or otherwise. These funds are equivalent to a loan by foreigners and should be regarded as a draft on the recipient country's stock of international reserves. Whether there is an outflow of gold or an inflow of foreign short-term loans, the country's net international liquidity will be reduced. The foreign short-term funds are a liability, can be withdrawn at any moment, and must be treated as a negative gold reserve.

Short-term capital movements of the disequilibrating kind should also be ex-

ings in excess of the amounts required by the holder in business operations in his own country are only temporary (seasonal holdings, or accumulations in anticipation of large capital expenditures), so that outflows of funds for liquid investments are likely to be followed by return flows within relatively short periods. Such capital flows could also be induced by relative changes in interest rates resulting from differences in the phasing of seasonal or cyclical fluctuations. In the latter case, however, it might take a relatively long time—most likely more than a year—before interest-rate relationships and capital flows are reversed.

There is no question that in the absence of restrictions, and with a minimum risk of loss arising from the conversion of a currency into another and back again, such capital flows for temporary investment in near-cash assets can be substantial. Being clearly temporary, there is a good argument for considering them separately in the balance-of-payments analysis and for computing a balance without such temporary and reversible transactions.

There may also be a valid argument that speculative capital movements of the disequilibrating type exaggerate the disequilibrium in the balance of payments, and that a proper measure of that disequilibrium should be derived by exclusion of capital flows induced by, and magnifying, that disequilibrium.

If one considers capital investments in securities equally affected by conditions quickly changing back and forth, one may include such investments also in the category of temporary and reversible transactions and disregard them in the analysis of the more fundamental balance-of-payments trends.

What these assumptions imply, however, is that such transactions occur within a group of countries with essentially homogeneous economies—countries essentially similar in economic development and structure, comparable in competitive strength, and in the economic policies of monetary and other governmental authorities. It can be easily seen, however, that under such conditions all disturbances in the international equilibrium will be essentially of short duration and

---

cluded from the balance of payments which we wish to use as a standard of the equilibrium rate. Such capital movements became very familiar during the 'thirties, in the form of capital flight and "hot money," and were due mainly to fear of exchange depreciation and of war. . . . In considering the balance of payments as a criterion of exchange equilibrium it is desirable, as a rule, to exclude all discrepancies which are due to such abnormal factors. . . .

Apart from international currency transfers and short-term capital movements, no exclusions are necessary or desirable for the purpose of our definition.

that movements of capital for liquid investment would be a part of the general pattern of short-term changes observable also in other transactions.

In the absence of a homogeneous environment, however, disequilibria can be more persistent as a result of deeper-seated and longer-lasting differences between countries in competitive strength, attractiveness for investments for their own and other countries' savings, and in economic and monetary policies.[5] Under such conditions, capital flows for liquid investments can be persistently in one direction for quite long periods, and may reflect the same basic conditions as the balance on the other transactions, rather than different and separate phenomena.

A persistent excess of liquidity in a country beyond its requirements and relatively more stringent monetary conditions in other countries can lead to a rather continuous outflow of funds for liquid, or other, investments. The reason for such a condition may lie in a policy increasing monetary liquidity under conditions which discourage the use of such funds within the economy. The rise in monetary liquidity may, in fact, be the result of a policy designed to encourage potential borrowers in order to stimulate the domestic economy. If the economy does not absorb the additional liquidity, however, and the excess is moved abroad, it reflects a rather fundamental difference between this and other countries, not a temporary condition which may be disregarded in balance-of-payments analysis and statistical presentation.

Likewise, if a government is reluctant to stem the outflow of capital by reducing internal monetary liquidity, because such a policy would also result in a curtailment of domestic economic activity below the level which productive resources (particularly the labor supply) in the country would permit, it is probable that there is a rather fundamental disequilibrium in the economy. A capital outflow under such conditions is not an ephemeric and temporary sideline in the international transactions of that country, but rather strong evidence of a more fundamental condition or development. While policies raising short-term interest rates are perhaps feasible and effective to stem or reverse capital flows for liquid and short-term investments between economically homogeneous countries, they are hardly appropriate to correct more fundamental disequilibria. Very strong actions may afford temporary balance-of-payments relief, but at the cost of a slowdown

[5] Nurske, *op.cit.*, p. 8, writes: "In particular, we must include [in the balance of payments for the purpose of measuring the equilibrium rate] all capital movements relating to international investment."

in domestic investments, and this slowdown could in the longer run reinforce the more fundamental difficulties.

Whether short-term capital flows reflect only temporary circumstances or more fundamental conditions cannot always be detected at the time when they occur. This can only be determined from data covering a longer period of time. And, since short-term capital flows are influenced by factors—political as well as economic—which also affect other transactions, it seems best in the balance-of-payments analysis to consider them in the same way as other transactions, separating as far as possible those which are believed to be temporary, but not treating the entire category a priori as necessarily and always temporary and quickly reversible.

The following tabulation shows the results of various tests applied to the international transactions of the United States, to determine whether the movements of U.S. short-term capital were, in fact, more volatile and more closely related to short-term changes in the overall balance, than the balances of various other types of transactions. The comparisons are based on seasonally adjusted data for the 49 quarters from the beginning of 1950 through the second quarter of 1962.

SOME VOLATILITY MEASURES OF BALANCES IN VARIOUS TYPES OF TRANSACTIONS (AFTER SEASONAL ADJUSTMENT) BASED ON QUARTERLY FIGURES FOR THE PERIOD 1950 THROUGH THE SECOND QUARTER OF 1962

	Average quarterly changes (millions of dollars)	Number of changes in direction of movements	Number of periods in which balances paralleled change in net liquidity
Balance on:			
Goods, services, remittances and pensions	222	17	37
Government grants and capital, net of loan repayments	144	22	27
Direct and long-term portfolio capital, assets and liabilities	196	31	34
Short-term investments, assets and liabilities (excluding liquid liabilities)	97	25	29
Errors and Omissions	165	31	23
Over-all balance (change in net liquidity)	344	27	xx

Using average quarterly changes as a measure, it may be observed that the net changes in short-term capital transactions (excluding the liquid dollar holdings of foreigners) average lower than those of the other balances shown here. Movements in short-term capital transactions changed direction during that period significantly less often than balances on other capital transactions. Although these measures reflect only some of the aspects of this problem, they do not indicate that short-term capital movements were more volatile than the balances on other transactions.

Nor do the figures indicate that they were more frequently associated with parallel changes in the net liquidity balance than the balances on the other transactions shown in the table. In 29 quarterly periods, out of the total of 49, short-term capital movements paralleled the changes in the liquidity balance; in 20 periods they moved in opposite directions. The frequency of parallel movements was less than for the balances on other capital movements, 34 out of 49, and on goods and services, 37 out of 49. Thus, short-term capital movements do not appear to have been the major factor in the changes in the net liquidity balance over the period as a whole, but this does not exclude the possibility that they were a major factor in certain periods, just as other transactions were in other periods.

(b) Errors and Omissions

"Errors and Omissions" in the balance-of-payments compilations appear to be somewhat more volatile than short-term capital movements, but since it is not known what is represented by this figure, it would not be compatible with careful analysis always to subtract it from the change in net liquidity and consider the resulting balance a reliable indication of the longer-run balance-of-payments trend.

"Errors and Omissions" are a residual difference between estimated or compiled credits and debits which in principle should be equal. The fact that the sum of all credit items seldom equals the sum of the debit items may be due to errors in data for those transactions which are either obtained from primary sources or are estimated, or to the lack of information on other transactions. In some instances the differences may result from the recording of the corresponding credit and debit items of transactions in different time periods, as for instance if the clearance of checks extends over the end of one period into the next, and the credit to the recipient is recorded before the debit to the payer. This could be important at the end of the year or at the end of June, when large payments are usually due. Transactions for which data are now not known or estimated include several types of services transactions, as well as some capital transactions. Errors may, of course, be found in all figures.

Although continuing efforts are being made to improve the data and to plug the gaps, problems in separating domestic from international transactions, the large variety of international transactions, their continuous changes as new conditions develop, and the difficulties in finding those who are engaged in such transactions and to obtain the proper data from them, sometimes open up as many as, or more, new problems in the compilations of these figures than are being solved.

Estimates can in some cases be made on the basis of samples, provided that some over-all totals are available by which the samples can be blown up. In the case of some services transactions, and income on investments, this is being done. For capital transactions it cannot be done, however.

Transactions for which data are not available, but which are estimated to be relatively steady, should not contribute to the major short-term fluctuations in the "Errors and Omissions." Other transactions may be responsible for the larger but more persistent changes, and still others for the quick oscillations. The latter are most likely to be due to unrecorded capital movements or lags in the recording of one of the two sides of major transactions, as mentioned earlier. The capital movements could consist of some which involve short-term claims or liabilities, but they could also reflect transactions in securities, particularly through nominees or directly through foreign brokers, for which data are not available. Experience has shown, however, that frequently large transactions which were supposed to be reported have been omitted from reports or reported incorrectly and initially resulted in "Errors and Omissions." Although in many cases appropriate corrections were made when the errors were discovered, in some cases they may have remained in the figures.

During the postwar period until the beginning of 1960, "Errors and Omissions" were on balance mostly credits, indicating that either debits were overstated in the compilations or credits were missing. The latter is probably more likely. Such missing credit transactions could have been receipts on various services transactions, and capital inflows from abroad, a large part of which may have come in violation of exchange controls of other countries, to increase earnings or to escape risks of restrictions imposed on the use of the capital or of currency devaluations.

In 1960, "Errors and Omissions" changed rather abruptly to net debits, approximately in the same magnitude as the average net credits during the preceding ten years. Because this change coincided with a large increase in the outflow of short-term capital, it was concluded that the shift in "Errors and Omissions" also reflected short-term capital movements. The conclusion was further strengthened by the recurrence of a large short-term capital outflow and net debits in "Errors and Omissions" in 1961.[6]

It is entirely possible that the shift in "Errors and Omissions" in 1960 reflected in part large outflows of capital. The fact that the balance continued to consist of large net debits in 1961 and in 1962 suggests, however, that more fundamental developments had taken place, and that the 1960 shift was not merely a temporary and quickly reversed phenomenon.

Quarterly changes in "Errors and Omissions" during the period from 1960 through the second quarter of 1962 paralleled those in short-term capital in 7 out of 10 quarters, but in 2 of these 7 the movement in one of the series, while parallel, was relatively very small. Movements paralleling those in long-term portfolio capital and direct investments were nearly as frequent during that period.

Furthermore, in 1962 recorded short-term capital outflows declined sharply, while (for the year as a whole at least) the debit balance in "Errors and Omissions" increased further.

A very large part of the short-term capital outflow in 1960 and 1961 was to Japan, and the decline in such capital outflows to Japan was a major factor in the decline in total short-term capital outflows in 1962. Unrecorded capital outflows are not likely to have been to Japan.

One of the factors accounting for the shift in unrecorded transactions in 1960 may have been a diversion of foreign capital—which during the 1940's and 50's had come to the United States largely without being recorded—to other countries, primarily in Europe. This would have reduced unrecorded credits for the United States. Unrecorded capital outflows since 1960 may have been purchases of European securities directly through foreign brokers and unrecorded direct investments, both motivated by the fast growth in European economies and the related higher current yields or anticipated capital gains. Some capital may also have moved to Canada, perhaps for deposit in Canadian

[6] For an extensive discussion of "Errors and Omissions" and their relation to other items in the U.S. balance of payments, see Philip W. Bell, "Private Capital Movements and the U.S. Balance of Payments Position," in *Factors Affecting the United States Balance of Payments,* a compilation of studies of the Joint Economic Committee (Government Printing Office, Washington, 1962).

banks. Deposits in Canada are not always recorded, since those who should report them do not always consider them foreign, particularly if they are denominated in U.S. dollars. Such deposits may have been attracted by higher interest rates, and sometimes by tax advantages. Unrecorded outflows of foreign capital may also have contributed to the net debits in "Errors and Omissions."

It is by no means certain, however, that capital movements accounted for all of this shift. International competition was greatly intensified in the markets for goods and services, and expenditures related to sales promotion probably increased. Such transactions are currently not estimated. There is also a possibility that foreign expenditures related to government operations abroad, some of which escape statistical recording, increased.

(c) Transactions in securities

Another type of capital movement which is sometimes considered to be volatile and essentially short-run investment is purchases and sales of outstanding securities, and long-term bank loans. Gardner considers them part of the "footloose open-market capital" which should not be included in the "basic balance."[7]

Essentially the same argument applies to these transactions as to short-term capital movements. Among economically homogeneous countries capital flows through purchases and sales of outstanding securities may indeed move back and forth, depending on cyclical and other conditions which over the longer run should cancel out. This includes security transactions which are made for gains from fluctuations in capital values, for purposes of spreading risks through diversification of the investment portfolios, and for higher current incomes. Investors in countries with essentially homogeneous economies may be expected to move capital for some of these purposes in opposite directions, and for other purposes to alternate the direction.

Capital flows among countries which are not homogeneous may be preponderantly and for long periods in one direction only. Better prospects for capital appreciation and higher yields, resulting for instance from relatively faster economic expansion, may be one of the factors contributing to one-way movements. Other factors may be political, related to the risks of investments or uncertainties concerning the investors themselves.

Again, as in the case of short-term capital, it is only possible on the basis of experience to decide whether capital movements resulting

[7] *Op.cit.*, p. 198.

from security transactions are relatively temporary factors in the balance of payments, to be treated as such in the analysis, or whether they must be attributed to more fundamental and longer-lasting conditions. To decide a priori in favor of the former point of view certainly cannot be considered adequate analysis. In the United States' experience, transactions in outstanding securities have resulted in a more or less steady net outflow of capital over the last few years, indicating that more enduring rather than temporary conditions were responsible for it.

3. *Distinguishing Autonomous and Compensatory Transactions*

The measurement of changes in net international liquidity is not the only concept used as a focus in the analysis of balance-of-payments compilations.

Some analysts prefer to separate from all foreign transactions those which they define as compensatory from those which they consider autonomous. Perhaps a quotation from an article by Walter R. Gardner may indicate best the ideas behind this concept.

.... When we speak of surplus or deficit, we must be referring to a portion only of the balance of payments. We can have a trade surplus or deficit. We can have a similar gap in goods and services; or in the goods, services, and international transfers that make up the current account. A deficit in the current account must always be matched by a surplus in the capital account, and vice versa. All these accounts have their significance for different purposes; but when we speak of the surplus or deficit that moves the exchange rate of a country around and forces the monetary authorities to take financial action to keep it within the support points, we are talking of something much broader. We are talking of the miscellany of merchandise, service, and capital transactions undertaken because of the profit to be made or because of political or other ends that are sought for reasons of their own. If this great aggregate of what might be termed autonomous transactions does not balance out, the exchange rate of the country will be pushed up or down, and the authorities must supply whatever compensatory financing is required to keep the rate from moving outside the support points. Thus we have autonomous transactions above the line matched by compensatory financing below the line. The compensatory financing may take the form of a movement of reserves, or a drawing on the International Monetary Fund (IMF), or the use of ad hoc loans or other financing for the purpose. It is only as we draw a line of this sort and group above it the autonomous transactions, and group below it the compensatory financing that comes into play only because the autonomous transactions fail to balance, that we see what it is that is pushing the country's international exchange rate up or down and creating an exchange-market problem.[8]

Several problems arise from this approach in analyzing the balance of payments. The first is concerned with the validity of the concept, the assumptions, and the statistical material; and the second with the purpose which this type of analysis can serve.

Essentially, Gardner attempts to separate those items in the balance-of-payments compilations which have exerted a pressure on the exchange rate from those which measure the extent to which the monetary authorities had to intervene on the market to keep the exchange within the permissible limits.

The first assumption he makes is that monetary authorities increase or reduce their international assets when they intervene in the exchange markets to keep their currency from moving outside the support points. This assumption is correct, but it does not follow that whenever monetary authorities intervene in the market they do it for that purpose. In fact, they also buy and sell international reserve assets for other reasons and under different circumstances. The authorities are not merely passive bystanders satisfied to leave the size of their reserve holdings to the fate of the exchange market. They are concerned about their external liquidity if they manage their affairs properly, and will attempt to raise reserves, if they are deemed too low, by buying reserve assets long before their own currency reaches the upper limit. Liquidity, as has been pointed out before, is not simply a by-product of other business operations. Changes in liquidity, consequently, are not necessarily the compensatory part of other transactions, but can be—and in the longer run are even likely to be—as autonomous a motivation as those underlying other transactions.

Purchases and sales of international reserve assets by the monetary authorities may also be motivated by their desire to influence the domestic credit supply in their country. In some foreign countries, private banks hold large amounts of foreign-exchange assets—mainly dollars— as part of their secondary reserves, because the supply of similar liquid assets and currency in their own country is too limited and their central bank is always prepared to purchase dollars. A tightening

---

[8] "An Exchange-Market Analysis of the U.S. Balance of Payments," *ibid.*, p. 196.

in official reserves, in these countries, will induce the private banks to sell their most liquid and lowest-yield assets—that is, their dollar assets—to their central bank. Such policies can, and have been, supplemented by special arrangements between central banks and commercial banks in some of the major foreign countries, under which the central banks have lent dollars at special rates or sold them with special repurchase agreements. Dollar holdings of the central banks and the commercial banks have been affected by changes in these agreements, quite independent of changes in the exchange rates of the currencies of these countries.[9]

While purchases and sales of foreign-exchange assets by monetary authorities can be both compensatory and autonomous, compensatory actions can also take other forms. Monetary authorities can react to pressures on the exchange market by changing domestic credit policies, and some countries have changed even taxes or tariffs. If these policies are effective, no clue may be found in the official-reserve changes as to whether pressures on the exchange rate have existed or not. Even if, as a result of such measures, a decline in reserves has stopped or a rise been induced, no conclusions can be drawn from these movements in the reserves with respect to the underlying and "autonomous" demand for, and supply of, foreign exchange and whether or not the potential pressures on the exchange rate (in the absence of restrictions on credit or directly on foreign expenditures) have been relieved. Where the exchange rate is not fixed, pressures on it will result in changes in the rate, but not necessarily in changes in reserve holdings. In all these cases such pressures will not be reflected in the balance-of-payments compilations.

Furthermore, compensatory transactions do not have to be limited to the monetary authorities. Private transactions can be compensatory and induced by exchange-rate changes, particularly if these changes are considered temporary, or they can be induced indirectly by the monetary authorities themselves—for instance by credit policies, or

[9] As was pointed out earlier, changes in domestic credit policies by the Federal Reserve System would have much less effect on the supply of reserve assets of our monetary authorities, since secondary reserves of our commercial banks consist entirely of domestic assets which would either be liquidated or built up. Actually, the same kind of assets are used for this purpose by foreign as well as domestic banks; there is no difference between them in that respect. The difference is that these assets are domestic for our banks (and purchases or sales are domestic transactions which do not appear in the balance of payments) while they are foreign for foreign banks (and purchases and sales do appear in the balance of payments of their country, as well as in our balance of payments).

63

forward purchases and sales, or lending of foreign exchange. When indirect methods are used by the monetary authorities to counteract pressures on the spot-foreign-exchange market, those transacting the foreign business may have as their primary purpose the gains from the sales or purchases of assets abroad, while at the same time the monetary authorities have as the primary purpose of their actions the achievement of changes in their liquidity position. But whose action is compensatory: the central banks which use private commercial banks as their instrument, or the commercial banks which act out of self-interest but under conditions established by the central banks, so that their actions serve the goal of the central banks' policy?

To distinguish an autonomous from a compensatory transaction presupposes an ability to determine motivations. Even that would not be realistic, because the motivations of those whose actions are actually recorded often only reflect the motivations of the authorities. The concept that the focus of balance-of-payments analysis should be "compensatory financing that comes into play only because the autonomous transactions fail to balance" is based on a highly over-simplified picture of international transactions. Further thought shows this concept to be neither theoretically nor statistically applicable to current conditions. The statistical problem is further complicated by the fact—which has already been pointed out—that large amounts of foreign official balances are held in the United States through commercial banks and appear in U.S. statistics as liabilities to foreign private banks.

The "compensatory financing" concept cannot be used in the analysis of the balance of payments of many foreign countries, and even less the balance of payments of the United States, precisely because of the role of the dollar as an international medium of exchange and a reserve asset. If dollars are transferred from one foreign country to another, they may shift from private to official holdings or vice versa. This will depend upon institutional arrangements and credit, or other, policies of the respective monetary authorities. Transfers of dollars between foreign countries result from their transactions with each other, not with the United States. Shifts of dollars between private and official accounts, within the same country, or through transactions between foreign countries, need not be related at all to the balance of payments of the United States or the exchange value of the dollar. Our role is merely that of a bank crediting one account and debiting another. What seems more appropriate to watch is whether the total of all foreign accounts here increases or declines.

Even if it were possible to distinguish between autonomous and compensatory transactions, one might ask what purpose would be served by an analysis of the balance of payments from this point of view. It would tell the monetary authorities that they had met pressures on the exchange market by purchasing or selling foreign-reserve assets and what the other transactions were at that time, but would fail to draw their attention to situations in which international transactions were balanced by means which in the longer run could not be continued. This failure would materially reduce the value of balance-of-payments analysis as a policy guide, because it would deprive the monetary authorities of the opportunity to take corrective actions in anticipation of reserve losses, in time for such actions still to be constructive, and it would also fail to alert the public that such actions were needed. This could be detrimental in any country, but even more so in the United States, the reserve-currency country whose large liabilities are quite liquid and constitute the reserve assets of other countries.

4. Differentiating between "Basic" Transactions and Those "Sensitive to Monetary Policies"

Hal B. Lary recently introduced the concept of "sensitivity to monetary policy" as a means of classifying international transactions.[10] He assumes that the transactions which are sensitive include (1) gold and convertible currencies held by the monetary authorities, (2) liquid liabilities to foreign and international monetary authorities, (3) liquid liabilities to private holders, including banks, (4) U.S. private short-term assets, and (5) unrecorded transactions. The other transactions are classified as "basic" transactions.

The balances on the two groups of transactions are, of course, equal with opposite signs. The "basic" transactions are said to be influenced "chiefly by general economic forces" and "tend to be slow to adjust. . . . their combined behavior provides a measure of the adequacy of the country's competitive strength and its 'capability to defend the exchange value of the dollar' " (p. 149).

[10] Hal B. Lary, *Problems of the United States as World Trader and Banker* (Princeton: Princeton University Press for the National Bureau of Economic Research, 1963), Appendix A, pp. 137ff.

The difference between Lary's selection of the type of transactions best suited to provide the focus for balance-of-payments analysis and as a guide to policy formulations of the monetary authorities, and those closest to measuring changes in net international liquidity related to the defense of the exchange value of the currency as outlined in this article, is the treatment of changes in privately held short-term assets abroad and in the balance on unrecorded transactions which Lary assumes to consist primarily of short-term capital movements.

Lary recognizes that most countries outside the financial centers "would not be able . . . to reduce their *total* foreign short-term indebtedness very quickly, or perhaps not at all," but he believes that the emphasis should be changed from the liquidity of the assets themselves to the sensitivity of the movement of funds to monetary policy. "The chief problem may be simply to prevent, or reduce, the further outflow of funds into such assets, irrespective of whether, or how quickly, the assets outstanding can be enticed home again."[11]

It was pointed out earlier in this article that private liquid funds held abroad under the effective control of the monetary authorities should be considered at least as secondary reserves available for the defense of the currency, but that under present conditions foreign assets of private U.S. holders do not qualify for that purpose.

If the availability of the outstanding assets to the monetary authorities were disregarded, and all private short-term capital movements combined with those in official reserves, an outflow of private capital resulting in a loss of official reserves would leave the "balance on basic transactions" unchanged, although a continuation of this situation would result in a progressive depletion of reserves. Clearly the situation would require actions by the monetary authorities not merely to stop the drain on the reserves, but to restore them to their prior level, provided the authorities considered that level the most desirable under prevailing conditions. What matters to the monetary authorities, therefore, is not merely their power to stop that outflow, but also the control over the assets themselves—that is, their power to force the holders to liquidate them and, directly or indirectly, to transfer the foreign-exchange resources to the official reserves.

There may be situations in which an outflow of private capital is clearly temporary and a resulting loss in official reserves can be expected to be reversed within a relatively short period. A proper analysis of international transactions should allow for that. As indicated earlier

[11] *Op.cit.*, pp. 150-151.

in this article, however, it cannot automatically be assumed that all "short-term" capital flows are temporary. Neither can it be assumed that all temporary and quickly reversible changes in the balance must be due to short-term capital movements. There are other transactions which can be relatively quickly reversed.

If the official reserves have been reduced as a result of transactions which are not likely to be reversed within a reasonable period, the monetary authorities, regardless of the transactions involved, will have to take policy actions to restore their reserves. If privately held foreign assets are not liquidated in response to monetary policy the surplus will have to be achieved on other transactions. It cannot be assumed a priori, as Lary's suggestion implies, that the restoration of the reserves which have been depleted by movements of "short-term" capital can be achieved through policies whose effect will be concentrated primarily on short-term capital flows and will result in their reversal, while reserves which have been depleted through other transactions will be restored through policies designed to achieve a surplus on these other transactions. Aside from the difficulties in assigning a cause-and-effect relationship between changes in reserves and specific foreign transactions, it is difficult to conceive of monetary policies which are designed to concentrate their effect on one type of transaction rather than another. (In this respect monetary policies differ from such specific policies as quotas, tariff changes, or restrictions on other transactions.)

Which transactions will be affected most by the policy actions of the monetary authorities will depend upon the sensitivity of the transactions, that is, upon the marginal costs which changes in the transactions may create. These costs will depend upon many and varying factors, including institutional conditions. The transactions which respond to the policy actions of the authorities will not necessarily be the same, therefore, as those which were responsible (if, indeed, such responsibility can be established) for the changes in the reserves which the monetary authorities want to correct.

In other words, a decline in reserves resulting from short-term capital outflows may require policies resulting in changes in other transactions to restore the reserves, and these policies may not differ from those appropriate in cases of reserve losses caused by other transactions. The policies have to affect future transactions to achieve the policy goals; they cannot necessarily be designed to affect the same transactions that caused the conditions which required the policy changes.

It would not be logical, therefore, to classify *ex post* transactions on the basis of *ex ante* policy problems, unless the transactions themselves provide the means to meet the problems.

The distinction, proposed by Lary, of "basic transactions" from those "sensitive to monetary policies" would be similar to the concepts developed in this paper, provided this "sensitivity" were strong enough so that privately held assets abroad could, in fact, be available to the monetary authorities, with the result that an increase in such private holdings would strengthen the effective liquidity of the monetary authorities.

Lary prefers to apply less stringent criteria, however. His proposal requires that all transactions included in the statistics of short-term private capital movements and reflected in "Errors and Omissions," regardless of the type of transaction or the transactor involved, even if the transactions do not strengthen the liquidity of the monetary authorities, be combined with official reserves in an analysis of the "basic" changes in the balance of payments.

Actually, Lary does not provide evidence that private "short-term" capital movements and "Errors and Omissions" are, in fact, significantly more sensitive to monetary policy and significantly less influenced by "general economic conditions" than other transactions. If the criterion of sensitivity is limited to the ability of such policies to reduce, but not necessarily to reverse, the outflow, it is not clear why longer-term loans by banks should not be treated similarly to shorter-term bank loans, and why a distinction should be made for corporations between their short-term capital transactions with independent foreign residents and similar transactions with their foreign branches and subsidiaries.

Even transactions on goods and services can react to changes in monetary policy, and more immediately, not only slowly and indirectly through income and price-effects, as Lary believes.[12] Costs and availability of capital can have a considerable and rather quick effect on inventory policies, and consequently on imports, and may also affect the decisions of corporate managements with respect to dividend disbursements of their foreign subsidiaries.

The other major consideration in connection with Lary's proposal, discussed here earlier, is concerned with the actual capability of the monetary authorities to use policies restricting capital flows, particularly if these capital flows reflect more than temporary differences between countries in the relation of capital supplies to requirements.

---

[12] See *op.cit.*, p. 149.

Lary recognizes this problem—"that is whether and to what degree credit conditions can be tightened, if needed to curtail the outflow of capital without running counter to domestic objectives and political forces,"[13] but apparently he does not consider that possibility sufficiently important to be reflected in his recommended balance-of-payments analysis.

Lary's assumption that all recorded short-term capital movements, as well as all unrecorded transactions, are sensitive to monetary policies raises, of course, the question how these transactions could continue to contribute to the drains on U.S. reserves over so many years. Lary's analysis concepts would imply that U.S. monetary authorities were not as effective in using their policy tools as they could and should have been, while the analysis explained in this article provides for the possibility that these transactions were indeed a reflection of very basic conditions, which made it extremely difficult for the authorities to change them.

5. *Using the Balance on Current Transactions as a Performance Measure and as a Guide to Policy Decisions*

Another view which is sometimes expressed holds that what matters more in the long run than changes in the balance on liquid assets and liabilities are the changes in the entire capital balance, encompassing both liquid and other assets and liabilities. Analysts holding this view consider an excess of exports of goods and services over imports, resulting in a rise in net foreign assets or a reduction in net liabilities, as an indication of the fundamental strength of an economy in its international transactions, and more significant than the changes in the country's net liquidity position.

The U.S. balance on goods and services was positive throughout the postwar period. If unilateral transfers are added to the debits and undistributed earnings of foreign subsidiaries of U.S. companies to the credits, the balance was also positive over that period. From 1951 through 1954 reinvested earnings amounted to $3.2 billion, or $800 million per year, and from 1955 through 1961 they totaled about $8 billion, or about $1.15 billion per year. These increases were, in part, however, offset by losses, such as those arising from the nationalization of U.S. enterprises in Cuba. At the end of 1960, U.S. direct investments in Cuba were valued in the statistics at close to $1 billion.

The rise in the size of U.S. liquid liabilities over the size of liquid

[13] *Op.cit.*, p. 155.

assets available to the monetary authorities thus was over the long run considerably more than offset by the rise in the value of other U.S. foreign assets over other liabilities. At the end of 1961, total U.S. foreign assets, including monetary reserves, were valued at $96 billion, while its total liabilities were $47.6 billion.[14] This compares with assets of $57.1 and liabilities of $18.4 billion at the end of 1950. Over that period net assets increased, therefore, from $38.7 billion to $48.4 billion. Most of the rise was concentrated in the first half of the period, however. At the end of 1957, net assets were about $47.6 billion, and the rise from then until the end of 1961, net of the losses in Cuba, was only $0.7 billion.

These relationships—it is pointed out—not only provide a better measure of the balance of payments than the changes in the balance on liquid assets and liabilities, but the growth in net long-term investments will also result in an increase in income on these investments and thus further strengthen the U.S. balance.

There are difficulties with these views: first, that longer-term investments abroad cannot necessarily be considered a substitute for liquid assets; and second, that a rise in long-term investments abroad cannot be considered separately, rather than as part of total investments, including those made within the country. As was pointed out earlier, liquid reserves are needed to meet differences in cash receipts and expenditures and to instill reasonable confidence in creditors that their claims can be met. Even in the case of a private enterprise fixed assets are not a substitute for liquid assets, partly because it is often—and particularly under emergency conditions—difficult to liquidate these assets for a reasonable price or borrow against them, and partly because the continued operation of the enterprise would be impaired if a major part of its fixed assets were liquidated.

This applies to the country even more than to individual enterprises. The large foreign assets of the United Kingdom did not provide an effective reserve in the early 1930's, when the pound sterling had to be devalued. Similarly, when the United Kingdom soon after the outbreak of World War II attempted to sell various U.S. subsidiaries of British companies, it was able to realize only a relatively small part of the amount at which they were valued. In order to raise funds in the United States, the British Government had to borrow here using

[14] The assets include the gold tranche in the IMF, the liabilities exclude dollar holdings by the IMF except for $800 million which represents a gold claim by the IMF on the United States.

securities as collateral, and even then the loans had to be obtained from the U.S. Government and were small relative to the then current valuation of the securities.

Some of the foreign assets accumulated by the U.S. Government during the postwar period through loans provided valuable help in meeting foreign expenditures in recent years, when the debtor countries agreed to repay these loans in advance of the amortization schedule. The major part of the outstanding loans—even if they are denominated in dollars—cannot be counted on to provide secondary reserves unless the debtor countries themselves have accumulated sufficiently large reserves and continue to have a surplus in their balance of payments. If these debtor countries develop balance-of-payments difficulties at the same time that the U.S. has such difficulties, it can hardly be expected that these countries will accelerate the depletion of their reserves by paying their debts to the United States before they are due. A large part of the foreign assets accumulated by the U.S. Government require repayment in inconvertible foreign currencies and are available only for limited purposes.

Privately controlled assets, as was pointed out earlier, are not available to the monetary authorities to meet balance-of-payments requirements under ordinary conditions. In extreme national emergencies this may be changed, but the question remains what their liquidation value under such conditions would be, or how valuable they would be as collateral for loans, and which countries would be in a position to provide the funds.

In principle, even more important is the question why only foreign assets should be considered in measuring the total solvency of the United States as distinguished from its financial liquidity. If this country should have to liquidate assets in order to supplement liquid reserves, its domestic assets are not only much larger than those held abroad, but a large part of them are probably more attractive to potential buyers or as collateral to potential lenders. There is no particular merit in the idea that only foreign assets are to be considered an offset to foreign liabilities or as potential reserve for emergencies.

An excess of foreign assets over foreign liabilities thus cannot be used to measure the availability of secondary reserves which can be mobilized by the monetary authorities (even if they had the political power to do so) in case they are required to defend the exchange value of their currency. Nor can the increase in net foreign assets necessarily be interpreted as a sign of economic strength of the capital-exporting country.

If the investments abroad are not offset by an equivalent positive balance on goods and services, the foreign transactions will result not only in a drain on the country's international liquidity position, but also in an underutilization of its domestic productive capacity, as domestic expenditures fall short of domestic earnings. In that case, savings are invested abroad rather than in productive facilities at home and some of the additional income of the capital-importing country is not spent on imports from the capital-exporting country but at home or saved. This type of situation would suggest that the capital-exporting country is—indeed—competitively weak rather than strong, precisely the opposite of what would be concluded from its export surplus alone.[15]

While in the longer run the foreign investments may add to the incomes of the domestic owners of the capital, the gain for the capital-exporting country as a whole is likely to be less than if the savings had been invested domestically and resulted not only in higher incomes for the owners of the capital but also for other factors of production, particularly if these other factors are not employed to their optimum capacity. Likewise, income on foreign investments does not necessarily improve the balance of payments more than additional exports facilitated by domestic investments.

By the same token, a country does not become poorer if it borrows abroad in order to finance domestic investments, or if it sells foreign assets and uses the proceeds to build up its domestic assets. What matters in the short run is that the additional imports of goods and services do not exceed the capital inflow, and in the longer run, that the adverse changes in the balance on investment incomes are at least offset by favorable changes in the balance on goods and other services and still leave a part of the increment in total output available for domestic use.

An import surplus financed by an inflow of capital thus does not necessarily reflect a weakness of a country's economy. If its external liquidity does not change, or if it improves, it may—in fact—reflect

[15] For a more extensive discussion of the balance-of-payments relationships between competitively strong and weak countries under conditions of expanding and contracting demand, see Walther Lederer, "The Effects of Changes in Domestic or Foreign Demand on the Balance of International Payments," in *Public Policy* (Yearbook of the Graduate School of Public Administration, Harvard University, Vol. XI, 1961), edited by Carl J. Friedrich and Seymour E. Harris.

comparative competitive strength. Many foreign countries, however, have experienced balance-of-payments difficulties because they have not been able to attract sufficient foreign capital to finance the excess of their investments over their *ex ante* savings and have resorted to credit expansion to meet either private or public demands for investment capital.

Although the rise in the domestic assets of these countries may have exceeded the decline in their international reserves or the rise in their foreign liabilities, this did not provide them with the means to defend the exchange value of their currency or to protect them from ultimate devaluation. The reduction in liquid funds to finance long-term investments is one of the most common causes of financial insolvency of business enterprises, and it can equally well be a cause for a country's inability to maintain the exchange value of its currency.

In the case of the United States, the large net outflow of capital in recent years did not result in an equivalent surplus on goods and services, and did not occur while domestic productive resources were employed at the point of their optimum utilization. There is room for question, therefore, whether either the surplus on goods and services, or the rise in net foreign assets can be viewed as signs of economic strength and whether either of these measures, taken by itself, can provide a valid interpretation of the state of the economy in its international relationships. A close analysis of the factors leading to the net capital outflow is more likely to lead to a different—and probably more realistic—diagnosis, similar to the one suggested by the changes in net international liquidity.

This brings us back to the discussion at the beginning of this article. The balance of international payments is needed primarily as a guide to economic and monetary authorities for preventing financial insolvency of the country. To meet this purpose, it should measure changes in international liquidity and provide the data needed to determine whether these changes are due to special factors or whether they reflect deeper-seated economic conditions or developments which can be corrected only through adjustments in prevailing policies.

PUBLICATIONS OF THE
INTERNATIONAL FINANCE SECTION

The International Finance Section publishes at irregular intervals papers in three series: ESSAYS IN INTERNATIONAL FINANCE, PRINCETON STUDIES IN INTERNATIONAL FINANCE, and SPECIAL PAPERS IN INTERNATIONAL ECONOMICS. All three of these may be ordered directly from the Section.

Single copies of the ESSAYS are distributed without charge to all interested persons, both here and abroad. Additional copies of any one issue may be obtained from the Section at a charge of $0.25 a copy, payable in advance. This charge may be waived to foreign institutions of education or research.

For the STUDIES and SPECIAL PAPERS there will be a charge of $1.00 a copy. This charge will be waived on single copies requested by persons residing abroad who find it difficult to make remittance and on copies distributed to college and university libraries here and abroad.

Standing requests to receive new ESSAYS as they are issued and notices of the publication of new STUDIES and SPECIAL PAPERS will be honored. Because of frequent changes of address and the resulting waste, students will not be placed on the permanent mailing list.

The following is a complete list of the publications of the International Finance Section. The issues of the three series that are still available from the Section are marked by asterisks. Those marked by daggers are out of stock at the International Finance Section but may be obtained in zerographic reproductions (that is, looking like the originals) from University Microfilms, Inc., 313 N. First Street, Ann Arbor, Michigan.

ESSAYS IN INTERNATIONAL FINANCE

† No. 1. Friedrich A. Lutz, International Monetary Mechanisms: The Keynes and White Proposals. (July 1943)
† 2. Frank D. Graham, Fundamentals of International Monetary Policy. (Autumn 1943)
† 3. Richard A. Lester, International Aspects of Wartime Monetary Experience. (Aug. 1944)
† 4. Ragnar Nurkse, Conditions of International Monetary Equilibrium. (Spring 1945)
† 5. Howard S. Ellis, Bilateralism and the Future of International Trade. (Summer 1945)
† 6. Arthur I. Bloomfield, The British Balance-of-Payments Problem. (Autumn 1945)
† 7. Frank A. Southard, Jr., Some European Currency and Exchange Experiences. (Summer 1946)
† 8. Miroslav A. Kriz, Postwar International Lending. (Spring 1947)

† 9. Friedrich A. Lutz, The Marshall Plan and European Economic Policy. (Spring 1948)

† 10. Frank D. Graham, The Cause and Cure of "Dollar Shortage." (Jan. 1949)

† 11. Horst Mendershausen, Dollar Shortage and Oil Surplus in 1949-1950. (Nov. 1950)

† 12. Sir Arthur Salter, Foreign Investment. (Feb. 1951)

† 13. Sir Roy Harrod, The Pound Sterling. (Feb. 1952)

† 14. S. Herbert Frankel, Some Conceptual Aspects of International Economic Development of Underdeveloped Territories. (May 1952)

† 15. Miroslav A. Kriz, The Price of Gold. (July 1952)

† 16. William Diebold, Jr., The End of the I.T.O. (Oct. 1952)

† 17. Sir Douglas Copland, Problems of the Sterling Area: With Special Reference to Australia. (Sept. 1953)

† 18. Raymond F. Mikesell, The Emerging Pattern of International Payments. (April 1954)

† 19. D. Gale Johnson, Agricultural Price Policy and International Trade. (June 1954)

† 20. Ida Greaves, "The Colonial Sterling Balances." (Sept. 1954)

† 21. Raymond Vernon, America's Foreign Trade Policy and the GATT. (Oct. 1954)

† 22. Roger Auboin, The Bank for International Settlements, 1930-1955. (May 1955)

† 23. Wytze Gorter, United States Merchant Marine Policies: Some International Implications. (June 1955)

† 24. Thomas C. Schelling, International Cost-Sharing Arrangements. (Sept. 1955)

† 25. James E. Meade, The Belgium-Luxembourg Economic Union, 1921-1939. (March 1956)

† 26. Samuel I. Katz, Two Approaches to the Exchange-Rate Problem: The United Kingdom and Canada. (Aug. 1956)

† 27. A. R. Conan, The Changing Pattern of International Investment in Selected Sterling Countries. (Dec. 1956)

† 28. Fred H. Klopstock, The International Status of the Dollar. (May 1957)

† 29. Raymond Vernon, Trade Policy in Crisis. (March 1958)

† 30. Sir Roy Harrod, The Pound Sterling, 1951-1958. (Aug. 1958)

† 31. Randall Hinshaw, Toward European Convertibility. (Nov. 1958)

† 32. Francis H. Schott, The Evolution of Latin American Exchange-Rate Policies since World War II. (Jan. 1959)

† 33. Alec Cairncross, The International Bank for Reconstruction and Development. (March 1959)

† 34. Miroslav A. Kriz, Gold in World Monetary Affairs Today. (June 1959)

† 35. Sir Donald MacDougall, The Dollar Problem: A Reappraisal. (Nov. 1960)

† 36. Brian Tew, The International Monetary Fund: Its Present Role and Future Prospects. (March 1961)

❉ 37. Samuel I. Katz, Sterling Speculation and European Convertibility: 1955-1958. (Oct. 1961)

❉ 38. Boris C. Swerling, Current Issues in International Commodity Policy. (June 1962)

❉ 39. Peter Lieftinck, Recent Trends in International Monetary Policies. (Sept. 1962)

❉ 40. Jerome L. Stein, The Nature and Efficiency of the Foreign Exchange Market. (Oct. 1962)

❉ 41. Friedrich A. Lutz, The Problem of International Liquidity and the Multiple-Currency Standard. (March 1963)

❉ 42. Sir Dennis Robertson, A Memorandum Submitted to the Canadian Royal Commission on Banking and Finance. (May 1963)

❉ 43. Marius W. Holtrop, Monetary Policy in an Open Economy: Its Objectives, Instruments, Limitations, and Dilemmas. (Sept. 1963)

† No. 1. Friedrich A. and Vera C. Lutz, Monetary and Foreign Exchange Policy in Italy. (Jan. 1950)

† 2. Eugene A. Schlesinger, Multiple Exchange Rates and Economic Development. (May 1952)

† 3. Arthur I. Bloomfield, Speculative and Flight Movements of Capital in Postwar International Finance. (Feb. 1954)

† 4. Merlyn N. Trued and Raymond F. Mikesell, Postwar Bilateral Payments Agreements. (April 1955)

† 5. Derek Curtis Bok, The First Three Years of the Schuman Plan. (Dec. 1955)

† 6. James E. Meade, Negotiations for Benelux: An Annotated Chronicle, 1943-1956. (March 1957)

† 7. H. H. Liesner, The Import Dependence of Britain and Western Germany: A Comparative Study. (Dec. 1957)

† 8. Raymond F. Mikesell and Jack N. Behrman, Financing Free World Trade with the Sino-Soviet Bloc. (Sept. 1958)

* 9. Marina von Neumann Whitman, The United States Investment Guaranty Program and Private Foreign Investment. (Dec. 1959)

* 10. Peter B. Kenen, Reserve-Asset Preferences of Central Banks and Stability of the Gold-Exchange Standard. (June 1963)

* 11. Arthur I. Bloomfield, Short-Term Capital Movements under the Pre-1914 Gold Standard. (July 1963)

* No. 1. Gottfried Haberler, A Survey of International Trade Theory. (Sept. 1955)

† 2. Oskar Morgenstern, The Validity of International Gold Movement Statistics. (Nov. 1955)

* 3. Fritz Machlup, Plans for Reform of the International Monetary System. (Aug. 1962)

* 4. Egon Sohmen, International Monetary Problems and the Foreign Exchanges. (April 1963)

* 5. Walther Lederer, The Balance on Foreign Transactions: Problems of Definition and Measurement. (Sept. 1963)